I SWEAR
THE MEANING OF AN OATH

I SWEAR

The Meaning of an Oath

By Joel Cohen
With Dale J. Degenshein

I SWEAR
The Meaning of an Oath

By Joel Cohen

With Dale J. Degenshein

Published by:

Vandeplas Publishing, LLC – October 2019

801 International Parkway, 5th Floor
Lake Mary, FL. 32746
USA

www.vandeplaspublishing.com

ISBN 978-1-60042-507-3

TABLE OF CONTENTS

DEDICATION

To the Memory of Eliezer (the Damascene),
A Paradigm for the Oath Taker

- Genesis 24

FOREWORD

It is not the oath that makes us believe the man, but the man the oath.
—Aeschylus

WAS AESCHYLUS CORRECT?

At some point in our lives each of us makes a New Year's resolution – a pledge, if you will, to do or to abstain from doing something; a change in some way from our current conduct. Perhaps, we'll be more attentive to our diet. Or we'll exercise more regularly. Maybe we'll refrain from cursing or from treating others derisively. Some of us will announce our resolution aloud. Others will keep it to themselves and simply adhere to their vow. Either way, the resolution or pledge, if not honored by us for a meaningful period of time, will typically have no consequence. The promise is to ourselves. If we tell people about it, others will likely laugh, probably along with us, about our "failure." We'll then wait until the next December 31st to, perhaps somewhat frivolously, make the identical resolution ("This time I will stick to it.").

But this book is not about New Year's resolutions. There are those in society who take oaths (some an affirmation) which by their very nature require adherence, whether for legal, ethical, or other reasons. Doctors are duty bound to heal, lawyers and priests to keep confidences, journalists to refrain from revealing sources, CIA Directors to keep the secrets, and presidents to act in the best interests of the country. Are these presumably non-optional vows broken by some?

Absolutely. We have seen it throughout history and, unfortunately, we glaringly continue to see it today.

A complete history, if there could ever truly be one, of those who have adhered to, or violated their oath, is far beyond the scope of this book. And so those who look to this book's title as suggesting that it is encyclopedic regarding the vast landscape of oath-taking would be disappointed – such a project is simply beyond the capacity of this author, or at least this project. Rather, I seek in this volume, through the prism of specific oaths that were taken by specific individuals, to raise broader questions and invite discussion about the different types of oaths that people take and the impact of their failure to comply with that oath – on them and on those who relied on that oath.

Physicians have an oath to heal the sick. We look at that oath through the lens of Samuel Mudd – was he performing his oath-bound obligation when he healed John Wilkes Booth hours after Booth murdered President Abraham Lincoln, or was he a co-conspirator? But the fact is that there are those who more blatantly, and unambiguously, violated their oath as a physician. Look at James Marion Sims, who lived from 1813-1883. He was a pioneer – the father of modern gynecology. He had significant works, all of which he perfected by operating without anesthesia on enslaved black women. Can there be any doubt that he violated his oath, no matter his vast medical contributions? Or Tuskegee – the 1932-1972 "studies" in which physicians failed to treat black men with syphilis so they could study the disease. And then there are the more muddled (for some) ethical questions surrounding physicians – the death penalty, abortion, euthanasia.

I write about Judith Miller – the journalist who went to jail for 85 days rather than reveal her source. Admittedly, I do not report the stories of other journalists who protected their sources to the end. Some of them we, as a nation, hold in high regard – Carl Bernstein and Bob Woodward never disclosed the identity of "Deep Throat," now known to be Mark Felt (the FBI's number 2 man), when they reported

Watergate. And *The New York Times* and *The Washington Post* never told the world that Daniel Ellsberg was the source for what we now know as the Pentagon Papers – Ellsberg turned himself in. Perhaps more controversially, should Julian Assange, the purveyor of Wikileaks, be permitted to hide behind his supposed oath as a journalist? If, of course, one considers him a journalist.

Can one "just follow the law" and therefore be freed from having to abide by his oath? Nazi soldiers, state officials, even judges took the "Hitler Oath" – their sworn oath of allegiance to the German Reich and to Adolf Hitler, rather than to the constitution of Germany. Many claimed they were "only following the law," but of course it was Hitler's laws that they were following. By making and following an oath to one man, did they violate their sacred duties as soldiers, officials, and judges?

Should the military court have credited Lt. William Calley, Jr.'s claim that he was "following orders" when he murdered 22 villagers during the Vietnam My Lai Massacre? (It did not, and he was convicted). Is an oath taken by a member of the Ku Klux Klan, or a militia group, the same as an oath taken by a member of the U.S. military? Does it matter if the oath taken requires a person to do (or refrain from doing) something the rest of the civilized world would conclude is utterly dishonorable?

Even when oaths are in place, are there exceptions? And what should they be? Can a psychiatrist, whose patient credibly suggests to her that he is considering blowing up a building, do nothing because of her oath of patient confidentiality? Should a journalist promise his source confidentiality, when his source is a ranking member of a terrorist organization?

Some may see all oaths as requiring an inflexibility that prohibits deviation – meaning, there are no exceptions or circumstances in which the oath-taker may properly depart from the oath's strict requirement. Others may see the oath as requiring a rule of reason where the oath-taker, in the fullness of time, may find it necessary to show obeisance or demonstrate unwavering fidelity to some other, perhaps higher-order, societal value.

This book is intended to make us think about the oaths we ourselves take. But it also asks the reader to consider, question, and understand oaths taken by other members of society, and the people who rely on the understanding that those oath-takers will strictly adhere to and be bound by what their specific oath requires.

For those followers of *Game of Thrones*:

Oaths and Vows and Prayers, all things said before Gods and Kings and people called our betters. They're all just words. They're all just promises. They're all just meant to be broken.

— *Ser (sic) Jaime Lannister, The Kingslayer.*

But that cynical analysis through the eyes of a fictional character is likely an unrealistic way to consider the issue. Many do adhere to their oaths – or at least, do the best they can.

To return to Aeschylus, is it the oath that makes the man, or is it the man that makes the oath? I believe each of us must come to our own conclusion, and I am hopeful this book provides a jumping off point for reaching those conclusions through dialogue, and perhaps providing the impetus for someone to author a defining work on this subject.

Joel Cohen
New York City, 2019

CHAPTER ONE
THE CIA DIRECTOR AND THE WITNESS

Richard Helms

THE OATH

Before we turn to the oath taken by a member of the Central Intelligence Agency, what exactly is the "Agency," as it is commonly called? From its website, we learn that the CIA is an independent agency responsible for providing national security intelligence to U.S. policymakers. It collects, analyzes, and disseminates intelligence information to top U.S. government officials.

It seems simple enough, except that the CIA does much of its work in secret. Often, only operatives who "need to know" have any knowledge of a particular program or activity. There are those who applaud the secrecy – and who would argue that the stability of the free world exists because of the CIA's covert actions. Others believe the public has a right to know and leak information so that the public can see the truth of the government's dealings. The CIA, however, does not sanction the release of confidential information, and the government has prosecuted those who leak.

The oath taken by those who work for the Agency seems clear enough:

I do solemnly swear (or affirm) that unless authorized in writing to do so by the Director . . . I will not disclose or reveal either by word, by conduct, or by any other means any information affecting the national interest or the national defense which I may obtain by reason of my employment . . . and I will forever keep secret any information so obtained by me ***

I do solemnly swear (or affirm) that I will support and defend the Constitution of the United States against all enemies, foreign and domestic; that I will bear true faith and allegiance to the same; that I take this obligation freely, without any mental reservation or purpose of evasion; and that I will well and faithfully discharge the duties of the office on which I am about to enter. So help me God.

Richard Helms, who worked in intelligence his entire adult life, took that oath. But he also took a second oath when he was questioned by the Senate in 1973, after he left the Agency. There, Helms answered the following question affirmatively:

Do you solemnly swear [affirm] that you will tell the truth, the whole truth and nothing but the truth so help you God [under penalties of perjury]?

When he left CIA service, Helms affirmed his obligations to the Agency. He promised that he would "never divulge, publish or reveal by writing, word, conduct or otherwise any classified information or any information, concerning intelligence or CIA that has not been made public by the CIA to any unauthorized person including but not limited to any future governmental or private employer or official without the express written consent of the Director of the CIA or his representative."

Do these oaths contradict each other? Was Helms placed in a position where, to uphold his oath as a CIA operative, he had to violate his oath to testify truthfully? And what price did he pay for having taken these oaths?

THE STORY

Richard Helms was a career intelligence officer. He worked for the CIA's predecessor, the Office of Strategic Services, during World War II, and continued his work when the CIA was created in 1947. He rose through its ranks until he served as the Deputy Director from 1965 – 1966. He was then appointed Director and served under Presidents Lyndon Johnson and Richard Nixon. While there can be little question that Helms participated in (and certainly was privy to) innumerable intelligence and counterintelligence operations, it is the CIA's involvement in Chile's presidential election in 1970 that is the subject of this story.

Let's step back. President John F. Kennedy wanted to make sure Chile remained a Latin American showcase for democracy – one that would stand in contrast to Fidel Castro's Cuba. While Kennedy, and later Johnson, were in office, Chile secretly received enormous amounts of U.S. aid through CIA maneuvers. Also, during the 1964 Chile presidential election, the CIA embarked on a propaganda and disinformation campaign, designed to make sure Eduardo Frei was the successful candidate.

Frei stood for social reform; his opponent, Salvador Allende, was (properly) portrayed by the CIA's campaign as a communist who would destroy the freedoms enjoyed by the Chilean people. Notably, it was also believed he would destroy the business dealings of Americans in Chile, and in particular, the dealings of International Telephone and Telegraph (ITT), at the time a major conglomerate in the fields of aerospace, transportation and telecommunications and majority owner of the Chilean Telephone Company. The CIA's effort was successful, and Frei was elected by a wide margin.

But Frei had difficulty putting some of his reforms in place. Those on the left were concerned that Frei had not pushed through enough of those reforms; some on the right were alarmed by what he had been able to pass. The result was a polarization in Chile's politics.

Fast forward. Richard Nixon took office in 1969 and was not about to follow a Kennedy-sanctioned plan of action. Nixon decided that the U.S. would not support Frei in Chile's 1970 election – Frei was too far to the left for his administration. Nixon decided to support Jorge Alessandri, a candidate more to his political liking but still one who would not turn Chile into part of a communist bloc, i.e., a country aligned with Russian and Cuban interests. Edward Korry, who had been U.S. Ambassador to Chile since 1967, warned the administration that early intervention would be necessary. There seems to be disagreement as to whether the CIA joined in that warning, or perhaps whether it joined in forcefully enough. In any event, it was not until six months before the election that the president's National Security Council Committee permitted the CIA to spend limited funds to influence Chile's election.

In the midst of this, Senator William Fulbright, who was chair of the Foreign Relations Committee, summoned Helms to his office. Fulbright knew the CIA had given assistance to Frei in 1964 and wanted to know whether the CIA was trying to sway the 1970 election. He warned Helms: "If I catch you trying to upset the Chilean election, I will get up on the Senate floor and blow the operation."

Six weeks before the election, it was clear that Chile's two leading candidates – Allende and Alessandri – were in a dead heat. Allende was an avowed Marxist – he was receiving support from Moscow and Cuba. Ultimately, Allende received 36% of the vote, barely two percentage points more than Alessandri. A third candidate, Radomiro Tomic, received 27%. The U.S. government, along with ITT and many Chilean people, panicked, plain and simple.

Nixon insisted that the CIA make sure Allende never took office. Under Chilean law, since no candidate won a majority of the votes, it was the responsibility of its Congress to choose between Allende and Alessandri. In the past, its Congress had always selected the candidate with the most votes. But the CIA and the U.S. had almost two months to try and sway that decision. As Helms's now-public notes reflect, he was authorized to spend more than $10 million as necessary, notwithstanding the small likelihood of success and the risks involved.

The CIA gambled on a questionable, and complicated scheme to keep Allende out of power – it required cooperation, persuasion and an infusion of money through the CIA's "contingency fund." But, it appeared that Allende and Tomic had made a secret deal to each back the other. It thus became clear that it would be impossible to keep Allende from taking office. Desperate, the U.S. tried its last best option, and participated – allegedly with ITT – in a Chilean military coup, one which was not successful. As to this order (eventually called "Track II"), it was known only by Nixon, Helms, Attorney General John Mitchell and National Security Advisor (later Secretary of State) Henry Kissinger. According to Helms, it was the most restrictive security order he received during his decades with the CIA.

Even though it had little chance of success from the start, Nixon, in particular, was furious when Allende was sworn into office. And he was especially furious at Helms. Rather than thank Helms for his determined efforts – and the fact that nothing about the U.S. government's efforts had leaked – Nixon and Kissinger were livid. That Allende took office was considered a failure by the Agency, and specifically, Helms. Helms, for his part, laid blame at the feet of the administration.

In February 1973, Nixon, who had just taken office for his second term, summoned Helms to Camp David and permanently removed Helms from his duties. However, Nixon and Helms agreed that Helms – a career public servant – would be appointed Ambassador to Iran.

As an aside, seven months after Helms was relieved of his position, the Chilean military staged a successful coup and Allende was not only removed from office, he killed himself (or perhaps it was an accident), just after he gave his farewell speech. Whether the CIA was directly behind the coup, or whether its funneling of millions of dollars to opposition groups for the prior three years made a difference – it is probably safe to say the CIA had a hand in Allende's downfall.

Let's put these actions into historical context. We have entered the early 1970s. Watergate was everywhere. Vietnam – how we got there and why we were still there – was being questioned. And the secrecy the CIA had long enjoyed as a necessary evil was being questioned. Politicians were no longer satisfied with clandestine operations being kept from them, and from the public. The rules were changing and the Agency, which had long been accustomed to being exempt from normal standards of accountability, could no longer rely on Congress to look the other way when the Agency acted covertly.

And this is where Helms's oath as a witness comes into play. During his Ambassadorship confirmation before the Senate Foreign Relations Committee in February 1973, Helms was questioned by Fulbright. Fulbright first questioned Helms about his CIA oath. Specifically, Fulbright asked Helms if he was "under the same oath that all CIA men are under when you leave the Agency and cannot talk about your experiences there?" Helms responded: "I think it would be a very bad example for the Director to be an exception." To Helms, no matter his disagreements with the president, his oath was sacred.

Two days later, the Committee again questioned Helms under oath, in a closed session. Helms swore "to tell the whole truth and nothing but the truth." At that point Senator Stuart Symington, who was a member of both Fulbright's committee and the Armed Services Subcommittee, asked three specific and direct questions:

Q: Did you try in the Central Intelligence Agency to overthrow the government of Chile?

A: No, sir.

Q: Did you have any money passed to opponents of Allende?

A: No, sir.

Q: So, the stories you were in that war [sic] are wrong?

A: Yes, sir.

Helms thereafter reviewed his testimony with the CIA's general counsel, who was somewhat concerned about Helms's categorical responses; however, Helms was comfortable. He believed that his 1973 testimony before the Senate was literally true. Symington – who was actually up to speed, except perhaps for Nixon's Track II order to intensify operations just before Allende took office – had asked the wrong questions, allowing Helms to answer as he did.

By 1975 – in the heat of the Watergate fallout and changes to the CIA – three federal commissions were formed, including the Senate Select Committee to Government Operations with Respect to Intelligence Activities, known as the "Church Committee," named for its chair, Senator Frank Church. It was tasked with determining whether the CIA exceeded its statutory authority and whether existing safeguards were in place. Covert actions to subvert foreign governments and assassination attempts on foreign leaders were being investigated for the first time.

Church was given access to all CIA documents, regardless of their classification. This included some of Helms's highly classified internal notes. Helms testified before the Church Committee for some hundred hours before it had completed its work. Ultimately, it concluded that "intelligence excesses, at home and abroad," were not the "product of any single party, administration, or man," but had developed as America rose to become a superpower during a global Cold War. It recommended some 96 legislative and regulatory initiatives to strengthen agency oversight. President Gerald Ford unsuccessfully tried to keep Church from publishing the report.

Sometime after the report was issued, Helms was warned by friends in high places that he was being investigated. While still in Iran, as Ambassador, he hired the single best trial lawyer of the day – Edward Bennett Williams – to represent him. Helms was not charged with leading the CIA in questionable activities. No – the Justice Department was determined to prosecute him on the basis of his responses to the Foreign Relations Committee when he was questioned on a response he gave to a different (open) committee chaired by Church in 1973 when Helms denied that the CIA had any contact with the Chilean military.

It soon became clear that the Justice Department not only had secret and top-secret documents, it also had the full details of Track II, Nixon's last-minute instructions to instigate a military coup in Chile.

Helms's many friends tried to stop the prosecution – if Helms lied, it was for the country and not for personal benefit. He was caught in the middle of a political firestorm and it was simply not fair to prosecute him for doing the same thing CIA directors had done for decades.

But in 1976, the Church Committee report had been issued and Jimmy Carter – having run on a platform that there would be no "dual" standard of justice (remember, Ford had pardoned Nixon) – was in office. The government had a problem – if it prosecuted Helms for perjury, it may well have to disclose additional classified information. Yet, dropping all charges wasn't an option. Helms, too, had to face the fact that a conviction would be personally devastating – loss of his pension and potential jail time. Williams and the attorney general ultimately made a deal; one which Helms did not want to take but did.

Helms would plead *nolo contendere* – literally "no contest" so that he did not admit or dispute the charge – to two misdemeanor charges of not testifying "fully and completely" and "accurately" before Congress (based on a lenient statute that is no longer in effect). Importantly, he would be permitted to keep his pension, he would not be required to serve time in jail, and he would not pay a fine. This was the lawyers' deal; the judge, however, did not have to comply.

The parties appeared before Judge Barrington D. Parker, chosen at random. It was assumed by the lawyers that Helms would appear and be sentenced immediately, but Parker had his own ideas.

Helms addressed the Court:

> I found myself in a position of conflict. I had sworn my oath to protect
> certain secrets. I didn't want to lie. I didn't want to mislead the Senate.
> I was simply trying to find my way through a very difficult situation in
> which I found myself.

Parker wasn't impressed. He adjourned the sentencing for a week, among other things, allowing the press to flood the courtroom. He imposed sentence: a $2,000 fine (the maximum) and two years in jail, to be suspended. But Parker did more than that; in a scathing lecture, Parker reminded Helms of his oath as a witness:

> You considered yourself bound to protect the Agency whose affairs you
> had administered and to dishonor your solemn oath to tell the truth . . .
> If public officials embark deliberately on a course to disobey and ignore
> the laws of our land because of some misguided and ill-conceived
> notion and belief that there are earlier commitments and considerations
> which they must observe, the future of our country is in jeopardy.
> ***Public officials at every level, whatever their position like any other
> person, must respect and honor the Constitution and the laws of the
> United States.

You now stand before this Court in disgrace and shame.

Once on the steps of the courthouse, Williams turned to the press:

[Helms] was sworn not to disclose the very things that he was being
requested by the Committee to disclose. Had he done so, he would have
sacrificed American lives, he would have sacrificed friends of ours in
Chile, and he would have violated his oath. Helms will wear this conviction like a badge of honor.

Helms agreed: "I don't feel disgraced at all. Had I done anything else,
I would have then been disgraced." Indeed, years later, in his book, *A
Look Over My Shoulder*, Helms explained why he testified as he did:

Aside from violating the presidential instruction, I had very quickly to
factor in the further possibility that my candid account of what went on
in Chile might leak – even from such a sequestered meeting. President
Allende was still in office. Any disclosure by me of the Agency's past
activities in Chile would certainly endanger the lives of those who
had cooperated with us at the time, as well as those who might still be
active in the anti-Allende efforts. I also remembered Senator Fulbright's
earlier promise: "If I catch you trying to upset the Chilean election, I
will get up on the Senate floor and blow the operation." Later, Fulbright
underlined his position by stating: "I pay no attention to the assertion
that CIA can only testify on operational matters before the Senate
Armed Services Committee."

Last, I had sworn to protect CIA sources and methods from unauthorized disclosure. To my knowledge only Senator Symington, among
those present at the hearing, was officially authorized to have access to
this information.

Like the captains of square-rigged sailing ships, I was caught between wind and tide in a narrow channel with no room to maneuver.

Helms's prosecution and plea were immediately subject to debate – and remain a source of disagreement to this day. Indeed, immediately after being sentenced, Helms went to a luncheon attended by some 400 retired CIA officers. News of the sentence had been on the radio. Helms was greeted with a standing ovation, and those attending filled a basket with cash and checks to pay Helms's $2,000 fine. So much was donated that Helms paid his fine and still had money to donate to the Agency's welfare fund.

In 1983, President Reagan awarded Helms the National Security Medal – a medal reserved to those who made distinguished and outstanding contributions to national security. Helms also served on Reagan's Commission on National Security. He died in 2002 and is buried in the nation's military cemetery at Arlington.

DISCUSSION

Richard Helms faced a conflict – that between honoring his testimonial oath "to tell the truth, the whole truth" and his CIA oath to "support and defend the Constitution of the United States, against all enemies both foreign and domestic," an imposing conflict to be sure. One is reminded of the legendary "lecture" given by Colonel Nathan Jessup (Jack Nicholson) to prosecuting attorney Lieutenant Daniel Kaffee (Tom Cruise) in *A Few Good Men*, in response to Kaffee's confrontational questions about whether Jessup had ordered a fatal punishment for a "substandard" marine. Read Jessup's words (written by Aaron Sorkin) in the context of Helms's world:

Jessup: You want *answers?*

Kaffee: I want the truth!!

Jessup: You can't *handle* **the truth!** Son, we live in a world that has walls, and those walls have to be guarded by men with guns. Who's gonna do it? You? . . . I have a greater responsibility than you can possibly fathom. You weep for Santiago and you curse the Marines. You have that luxury. You have the luxury of not knowing what I know: that Santiago's death, while tragic, probably saved lives. And my existence, while grotesque and incomprehensible to you, saves lives! You don't want the truth, because deep down in places you don't talk about at parties, you *want* me on that wall. You *need* me on that wall. We use words like "honor," "code," "loyalty." We use these words as the backbone of a life spent defending something. You use them as a punchline. I have neither the time nor the inclination to explain myself to a man who rises and sleeps under the blanket of the very freedom that I provide, and then questions the manner in which I provide it! I would rather you just said, "thank you," and went on your way. Otherwise, I suggest you pick up a weapon, and stand a post. Either way, I don't give a *damn* what you think you are entitled to!

Does the public want to know how the sausage is made, if you will? Better still, *should* the public know what the CIA has done over the years in the name of protecting America and, perhaps more to the point, how it accomplishes its goals? Think about post-9/11 activities. The public learned that the U.S. was torturing enemy combatants. People protested, outraged – to do such a thing violates the very values that makes America a great country. Others believed that any and all methods should have been used to make sure Americans were safe. Many people, however, tried hard not to know. Isn't that what

Jessup (Sorkin) was saying – people want to make sure it gets done, they just don't want to know how.

So is it preferable to have a public record made blurry by a government official, such as Richard Helms – viewed by most as an unyielding patriot? He deliberately kept the public in the dark by misleading a congressional committee about his actions, some of which people would consider sins, albeit sins committed in the public interest.

It is likely that one of the unwritten rules – duties – of a CIA director (and certainly during Helms's time) was to carry out the will of the president, often without the president's fingerprints on the action. In other words, the president had to have "plausible deniability." Regardless of whether Nixon's fingerprints were all over the debacle that was the 1970 Chilean election and the later military coup, was misleading the Senate and, significantly, the public, part of Helms's obligations as CIA Director? Did misleading the world serve his oath to protect the U.S. from its enemies?

Now, one might argue, who in America really cared about Helms's testimony about Chile? There was no internet; there wasn't even C-SPAN at the time of Helms's testimony. Isn't it possible that his testimony, had it been fully and completely truthful, would have appeared on the evening news and in the newspapers for a single day? Why would Helms's testimony about the political divide in Chile in the 1960s and 1970s and the CIA's role have been of interest? And if there was real concern about the public's knowing, why then didn't Helms ask to have his testimony sealed (this was, of course, during a time unlike today when most confidential information was far more likely to remain confidential)?

Was Helms's need to protect the president paramount? Was it the potential of political fallout? Or did he simply want to make sure that the full thrust of the CIA's actions remained under wraps? Truth can be dangerous. Transparency may not always be a valuable commodity in governance.

Should we allow leeway for government officials charged with keeping secrets in the public interest? It's a little hard to answer that question when applying 2018 standards to 1970 actions. The rules have changed, to be sure. Are we prepared, today, to look the other way at a CIA official who would lie to a congressional oversight committee about a plan (hypothetical, of course) to assassinate the president of a foreign power? Whatever actions the CIA might take or be knowledgeable about today, *testifying falsely under oath* about it would be absolutely verboten.

Now, Helms would likely say that he never lied – he just did not elaborate when senators asked the wrong questions. But, as we have evolved, so has the standard: the "coverup is worse than the crime." In other words, the perjury is worse than the clandestine efforts by agencies such as the CIA to engage in conduct the public might find reprehensible, such as torture in the wake of 9/11 or in ticking time bomb scenarios involving potential threats to our nation's domestic security. Could a Richard Helms survive today? Maybe, but he likely would not be applauded in the same way if he engaged in the same conduct now.

Thus far, in analyzing the Helms oath, we speak of the real politic of what occurred. Having straddled in government service a period when certain conduct on the part of the CIA was considered acceptable and when it was no longer so, the Justice Department decided that he would have to pay a price, inasmuch as lying, or at least misleading the Congress, was something Helms felt necessary to do. Meaning, the Department would accept a *nolo contendere* plea, rather than a guilty plea; a misdemeanor plea, rather than a felony plea; and a proposed sentence of probation, rather than a jail sentence on the part of the government would be viewed as a fair disposition of the case. Indeed, such a disposition of the case was offered Helms by the Department because, given the circumstances and the conduct implicated, the Department (and President Carter who authorized the plea) undoubtedly believed that the public would not decry the leniency.

That doesn't change the reality that Helms indeed violated his oath as a witness – even if the conduct under investigation by the Church Committee in 1975 may have been completely tolerable in the eyes of the body politic when committed. While Helms and his attorney would take the position that he was acting righteously in maintaining the secrecy, even when violating his oath as a witness, no one could reasonably argue that lying to or misleading Congress was acceptable conduct. The oath is the oath – whether one swears, or perhaps, "affirms under penalty of perjury" (so as to keep religious tenets out of the mix).

Lest it go unsaid, the practical meaning of an oath when taken before, say, a congressional committee, is far different than when the oath is taken by a witness in a litigation, civil or criminal. Testimony before a committee is largely political in nature – Congress takes testimony as a check against the executive branch or in support of findings needed to pass legislation. And in Helm's case, the pendulum was swinging from one administration to another, each with different tolerances for covert actions.

Testimony before a judicial tribunal, on the other hand, is required for factfinding needed to achieve a verdict for one party or another. Does that mean that testimony in one forum, as opposed to the other, is less serious and the oath therefore carries less gravitas? Absolutely not. Nonetheless, the public's view may be far different.

The public has little concern about an oath-taker's violation of his word that results in a particular way in a civil dispute, and perhaps likewise in a criminal dispute of little public moment. But the public may be more interested if some public interest is at stake, such as a hearing over a questionable protocol, for example, waterboarding.

Nonetheless, in some respects, the bigger question presented here is the meaning of the oath for the individual who violates it. Richard Helms, presumably, did not think twice about misleading the Senate. He believed that he was doing the nation's – at least the then-president's

– bidding by keeping, or at least trying to keep, the Chilean involvement *in times past* under wraps.

At bottom, Helms essentially argued that he had a higher duty than the oath he took as a witness – he swore to "protect and defend the Constitution against all enemies, foreign and domestic." Is that enough? Turning again to Aeschylus, is it the oath, or the individual who takes the oath?

CHAPTER TWO

THE LAWYER

Staples Hughes

THE OATH

Although it varies from state to state, the essence of a lawyer's oath, taken when one is admitted to practice law, is deceptively simple:

> I do solemnly swear (or affirm) that as an attorney and as a counselor of this court I will conduct myself uprightly and according to law, and that I will support the Constitution of the United States.

The oath requires upright adherence to law, and thus statutes, cases, and rules of ethics – professional conduct – are each subsumed within the oath.

One of the most imperative and challenging tests for a lawyer is that of confidentiality. It is easy to say there is an attorney-client privilege – if I tell my lawyer something, the lawyer can't repeat it. He must take it to the grave. It is easy to say lawyers must keep secrets. How else can they properly represent their client? After all, protecting the interests of their client is what a lawyer is legally and ethically obligated to do.

All true, but let's view these precepts through the prism of just one attorney whose confidentially-obtained knowledge seriously impacted the lives of others.

Imagine languishing in jail knowing, as in most cases perhaps only you as the defendant would, that you are totally innocent. Now imagine instead that you are a person who knows – indeed, is certain – that the man in jail for life didn't commit the crime at all, yet you can't tell a soul. Worse perhaps, you represent the man who committed the crime and do not, recognizing it would not be in his interest, even advise him to come forward to allow an innocent man to go free. The lawyer's oath is not so simple after all.

Lee Wayne Hunt – *likely* innocent of his crimes – had been in prison from 1985 until his death in 2019. While it is tempting to tell our story from the point of view of Hunt, we tell it from the perspective of Staples Hughes, Counsellor at Law, and attorney for Jerry Cashwell, who was by all accounts, a murderer, and *the* murderer in question. By the time you finish reading this story, you may understand and appreciate Hughes's predicament; you may even be appalled at his failure to have acted earlier than he did. But whatever you conclude, you may come to gain at least some insight into the difficulties lawyers sometimes face in acquitting their responsibilities to the law, their oath, and their own moral compass.

In 1986, Hughes was a public defender in North Carolina. Now retired, he was a very well-respected attorney. Hughes had been assigned to represent Cashwell, who had been implicated, along with Hunt and one other, in the brutal murder of Roland and Lisa Matthews. Their two-year old daughter had been in the house while her parents were murdered. Being too young to "talk," she was left unharmed, albeit orphaned.

Cashwell, represented by Hughes and two others, was convicted at trial, but because of a procedural error, his conviction was reversed. When the State decided to re-try Cashwell, he pleaded guilty to murdering the Matthews. He was sentenced to life plus fifty years, a sentence that, one supposes, would have said something to a parole board, had Cashwell ever come before it. But as to Cashwell, his sentence terminated in 2002, when he took his own life.

Hunt was tried for the same murders six months after Cashwell. They were co-conspirators, according to the prosecution – both present at the murders. There was testimony of bad blood between Hunt and Roland Matthews (Matthews had stolen marijuana from Hunt, who was going to "teach him a lesson."). A former cellmate testified that Hunt once told him, "all they had was just two dead bodies, no witnesses. They would never find the gun." There was also expert testimony about bullet-lead analysis to match bullet fragments to a box of ammunition belonging to Cashwell (and thus, according to the prosecution, Hunt). And perhaps as a final straw, Hunt presented a witness who testified that Hunt did not kill the Matthews. However, the witness was forced to reveal that he had made up his story because Hunt demanded that he do so – he was afraid of Hunt and lied for him under oath. Hunt was convicted and sentenced to two terms of life in prison. Another message to a future parole board, one supposes. Hunt tried to have his conviction overturned, to no avail.

But this is all background to the story of Staples Hughes. In 2004, after Cashwell committed suicide, and two decades after Hunt was convicted, Hughes called Hunt's attorney and said, in essence, "I know he didn't kill the Matthews." You see, back in 1985, Hughes and his public-defender co-counsel Mary Ann Tally (who later became a judge) met with Cashwell, their client. Cashwell told them confidentially that *he alone* had killed the Matthews. The details, the specifics, and the consistency of the story during the course of their representation of Cashwell made Hughes quite certain beyond any doubt that Cashwell acted alone. Not to mention Cashwell's admission to Hughes who described it this way: "If you were in the room, you'd have no question he was admitting and telling us the truth."

Hughes had no choice but to remain silent. Indeed, Hughes did all he could to represent his client. In presenting arguments to the court both at trial and sentencing, Hughes made carefully worded statements on his client's behalf. The lawyer's oath is complicated – while it doesn't allow an attorney to tell what was said in confidence by a client, it also doesn't allow a lawyer to make intentionally false statements. A fine line, to be sure.

When, in 2001 or 2002, just before Cashwell committed suicide and Cashwell told Hughes (and Tally) "You know, Lee Wayne's [Hunt] still out there," they told Hughes to remain silent. They were concerned that, if Cashwell admitted he acted alone, he would be denied parole. Counsel said, in effect, "That's Hunt's problem." Indeed, as Hunt's lawyers described Hughes's dilemma in papers to North Carolina's appellate court:

> [Hughes] was tormented from the very beginning by his knowledge of
> [Hunt's] innocence and his inability to reveal the information. Bound
> by the ethical rules in force at the time, by his personal feelings of loy-
> alty to his client, and by his knowledge that his client's version of the
> crime was more damning to the client than the State's version, Hughes
> did not even try to persuade Cashwell to admit sole responsibility. He
> even advised Cashwell to assert his right not to incriminate himself
> under the Fifth Amendment . . . when called to testify at [Hunt's] trial.

Hughes, himself, explained his dilemma in his submission to the disciplinary committee, discussed below:

> [Shortly before his suicide, Cashwell] started talking about his
> regret over what had happened to Lee Wayne Hunt. Ms. Tally and I
> immediately interrupted to tell him that Mr. Hunt's problems were
> Mr. Hunt's problems, and that [Cashwell] needed to worry about his
> own situation. In retrospect, I wish that I had let [Cashwell] share

his regrets with us. I do not know whether such an exchange would have led to his public disclosure that he was solely responsible for the crimes . . . This was an instance of the lawyering instinct overcoming an unusual opportunity to appropriately relate to a client directly as another human being in pain. . . I never considered that it might be in [Cashwell's] best interest to explore with him the option of disclosing the truth.

So, what was it that made Hughes conclude it was okay for him to call Hunt's counsel in 2004 and tell him that Cashwell had privately admitted to him that he alone committed the murders, and that Hunt was a total innocent? Two things – a case had just been decided in North Carolina which allowed disclosure of a *deceased* client's confidential communications in a criminal matter where, the court found, the public's interest outweighed the need for confidentiality; and of course, Cashwell was now dead. Truth be told, it is an extremely rare circumstance that a client's death releases the lawyer from the burden of the oath – indeed, the Supreme Court of the United States has specifically held in the case arising from the suicide of Bill Clinton's counsel and friend, Vince Foster, that an attorney (in that case, Foster's attorney, who was seeking to vacate his conviction) must take his client's confidences to the grave.

So when Hughes took the witness stand to testify on behalf of Hunt, the judge reminded Hughes of his obligations: "If you testify, I will be compelled to report you to the state bar." Plain, simple and direct. Hughes fully understood that if he testified to what his now-deceased client, Cashwell, had told him 20 years earlier, the judge would try to have his license to practice law – his very livelihood – taken away.

Difficult choice, but Hughes made it. He testified. Tally and one other who represented Cashwell at the time declined to testify unless the court ordered them to, citing their oath and their belief in the attorney-client privilege. The court wouldn't order them to testify but did allow them to submit sealed affidavits about Cashwell's confession, so that an appellate court could review what would have been their testimony.

But the judge did something in addition to reporting Hughes's behavior to the licensing authorities. He made the remarkable decision that because Hughes testified in violation of the attorney-client privilege and rules of ethics (all bound within the oath's obligation to "conduct myself uprightly and according to law"), he would not credit the testimony. It was inadmissible!

And as to Hunt – *The Washington Post* and *60 Minutes* did a joint investigation and reported the story in a 2008 *60 Minutes* story. Also, the bullet-lead analysis used to convict Hunt was no longer considered scientifically credible (a fact which the FBI admitted). So with all these factors, and Hughes's testimony (even if inadmissible), Hunt had to be freed, right? But, no, things didn't turn out that way. The courts determined that Hunt failed to demonstrate that he was "actually innocent" of the crime, in part because of his own statements and "admissions" to fellow inmates. Resultantly, his *habeas corpus* petition seeking to undo his conviction came too late. He died a prisoner.

As to Hughes, was what he did all for naught? It didn't get Hunt released. And he found himself defending his actions before a disciplinary committee, which after its own investigation has not pursued the judge's charges against Hughes. But even in that venue, Hughes explained his adherence to the oath: "I never considered disclosing the truth while Jerry [Cashwell] was alive. I believe that because he had some possibility of parole, if only as an elderly man, and because the truth would probably eliminate all hope of parole, I should not disclose the truth."

In other words, so long as there was *some* possibility, however slight, that Cashwell could go free, Hughes understood that his oath far outweighed any moral (perhaps) obligation to tell all that he knew, no matter how it weighed on him. Meaning, had Hughes come forward earlier and disclosed what Cashwell admitted to him while Cashwell was still alive, he would have been violating his oath; but Hunt might, at least theoretically, have been released from prison.

In teaching legal ethics to law students for many years, I would begin the first class of each semester asking my students to leave at the threshold all of the ethical, perhaps call it moral, training that they learned in the past from their parents, priests or ministers, rabbis or imams, or even, if it is the case, from Oprah. After all, the type of ethical training one receives in *the real world* may be profoundly different than the ethical precepts that lawyers are uniquely required to live by. How could it be possible for an "ethical" person who has somehow learned from an individual that he was the individual who committed a crime for which another stands falsely convicted – perhaps even destined to spend the rest of his life in jail – to remain mute? But yet, the lawyer's duty of confidentiality that is simply not imposed on non-lawyers has historically required just that: a lawyer is obliged by oath to take to his grave the secrets confided to the lawyer in the confessional of the attorney-client relationship (even if the lawyer learned what he learned in the context of that relationship, albeit not from the client directly).

So, the oath that the lawyer takes when he is admitted to practice law essentially requires that he follow the disciplinary rules that attach to practitioners of the law. Until relatively recently, the obligation to maintain confidentiality was absolute and across the board. For example, in the extreme case where the defendant wrongly convicted of murder faced immediate death, the lawyer for another man who (confidentially) confessed the murder to him – thus, being the only person beside the murderer who knows the truth – was obliged, without exception, to simply keep to himself what he knows despite the horrendous burden placed upon him by that ethical obligation.

The ethics rules have been liberalized somewhat. In most jurisdictions in the United States, lawyers faced with this situation – imminent certain death or even dire physical injury for the wrongly convicted – "may" (but not must) make the disclosure, i.e., "My client has confessed to me that he did the killing, not the defendant sitting on death row." So, now, in these jurisdictions, the lawyer can meet his ethical obligations by total silence – he needn't even urge his client to come forward and "do the right thing," which will obviously have potentially horrible consequences for him. Alternatively, the lawyer whose sense of moral duty impels him to disclose would be well within his rights. This, although one suspects that his decision to "hand up his own client" might have significant repercussions to his own ability to practice law when would-be clients might fear a lawyer "too willing" to betray a client's confidences.

Suppose, however, that a defendant is wrongly convicted of murder, but for some bizarre reason he is serving his life sentence at a minimum security prison. Quite clearly, even under the now-liberalized disciplinary rule, the lawyer would probably be obliged to keep to himself that his client has confidentially confessed his guilt that the defendant serving a life sentence for that very crime is innocent. There is, here, no reasonable concern of imminently dire physical injury for the innocent. In this case then, had Cashwell's lawyer, Staples Hughes, yielded to his personal code of moral behavior – that is, to not allow a totally innocent to languish in prison for something he didn't do while his confessing client was still alive – he would clearly have been subject to disciplinary action.

Hughes's circumstances, while unusual, are not singularly unique. In Illinois, Andrew Wilson, who was in jail for murdering two police officers, told his lawyers that he also killed a security guard. Yet, Alton Logan, and not Wilson, was convicted of killing the guard. Wilson's attorneys convinced their client to give them permission to tell what they knew *when Wilson died*. The lawyers signed an affidavit with what they knew and locked it away for 26 years until Wilson died. Unlike Hunt, Logan was set free.

But Wilson's lawyers occupied a somewhat different position on the rules which they were oath-bound to obey. They have said that, if Logan were subjected to the death penalty (rather than prison), they would have disclosed the truth then and there, the theory being that the rules allowed them to break confidentiality to save another from death. One of those lawyers, in a *60 Minutes* story about the case, was asked why he didn't just tell his client to tell the truth. His response, perhaps, well explains a lawyer's oath:

> The vast majority of the public apparently believes that [a lawyer must tell the truth], but if you check with attorneys or ethics' committees or you know anybody who knows the rules of conduct for attorneys its very, very clear – it's not morally clear – but we're in a position [] where we have to maintain client confidentiality, just as a priest would or a doctor would. It's just a requirement of law. The system wouldn't work without it.

Lest anyone conclude this dilemma is only found in criminal cases, let's look at the world of civil law. David Spaulding was 20 years old when injured in an automobile accident. He sued the two drivers. After the accident, Spaulding was examined by his own physician, who noted "the heart and aorta are normal." However, a neurologist retained by the defendants' attorney found that, in fact, Spaulding had an aneurysm, i.e., a dilation of the aorta. While it couldn't be determined whether the aneurysm resulted from the accident, in a boy of 20, it "is a serious matter as far as his life."

You are the lawyer for the defense. Do you tell the 20-year-old or his parents that he might have a serious condition, a life-threatening condition which will adversely, and seriously so, impact your own client's negotiating posture? Or do you make a quick deal so your client can save some money? What is your ethical obligation? In *Spaulding*, the lawyer did not tell; Spaulding found out about the aneurysm during a medical examination a few years later; and the settlement so carefully maneuvered by the defense avoiding disclosure was vacated – at 20, Spaulding was a minor and had the right to challenge the deal. But the court was clear – the defense counsel was under no legal or ethical obligation whatsoever to disclose what he knew when first negotiating settlement; and, indeed, and, certainly surprisingly to most layman, counsel did nothing wrong.

Let's modify *Spaulding* into a hypothetical. Imagine that a lawyer has a gigantic practice defending product liability cases for an automobile manufacturer – ABC Cars. An ABC Car air bag malfunctions, and a ten-year-old child suffers a serious, but not a seemingly life-threatening injury. The child's parents retain a not-so-great personal injury lawyer to sue ABC, and he does. The plaintiff's lawyer retains a low-end physician to examine the child's head for a possible concussion, which he finds – but nothing much more. The plaintiff's lawyer armed only with a low-end medical report, sees the case worth, say $50,000, which is what he seeks from ABC.

ABC's lawyer, as in every case, retains a forensic physician for ABC. His examination is far more thorough, and he finds that the child also suffered an aneurysm from the automobile accident. He reports what he found to ABC's attorney and in-house counsel who in turn reports it to ABC Cars' executive in charge of settling cases. He directs ABC's lawyer to settle the case promptly at the $50,000. He also *directs* ABC's lawyer to comply with his confidentiality obligations: "Keep your mouth shut about the aneurysm. Your exclusive duty, as well as that of the doctor you retained, is to ABC."

Let's put aside the pathologist's quandary. What about ABC's lawyer: he's being asked to sit on information that if kept secret, might potentially result in the child's death, or at least serious bodily injury. And he's basically told, in some way, that if he makes the unauthorized disclosure, that will end his retention by ABC, which represents, in this hypothetical, 75% of his legal practice. In the old days, before the rule was changed, the lawyer would be obliged to keep his confidence to himself at penalty of a lawsuit against him by ABC and disciplinary action for violating his client's confidence. But now, lawyers in most states have the option to disclose if imminent bodily injury is feared. Still, lawyers aren't *required* to disclose, however morally painful it might be to sit on the information.

Imagine, again, the duty of the oath. The lawyer's "oath" no longer *requires* the lawyer to sit on the information, but nonetheless *allows* him to remain silent. So, he is *allowed* to let his personal sense of morality prevail by disclosing and not be subject to disciplinary action; and, at the same time, he may risk impairing his ability to practice law at the level heretofore available to him by doing the moral (if not ethically required) thing. The oath, in some respect, has thus become meaningless, as the lawyer might go in either direction, particularly if he is independently wealthy. He can make the disclosure, and potentially lose his business opportunities with ABC (or other potential clients who will likely "go in another direction" fearful that he's "too moral for their tastes"). Or he can "ethically" take the direction his client directs and pursue a protocol of client-directed *omerta*.

So, let's review, assuming that the reader (and the author) are laypeople – with no obligations of an attorney's oath whatsoever attaching. We learn from the horse's mouth that he, the murderer, is the lone murderer, and that the accused is a *total* innocent. And assume, too, that we have no relationship whatsoever with him. Finally, assume that we are sentient human beings, caring people simply unwilling to bury our heads in the sand (saying "it's none of my business"). Is there any chance in the world that we would simply do nothing, and would even strongly encourage the actually-guilty murderer to maintain his silence given that it would harm him dramatically to do otherwise? Likewise, would we sit on our hands and keep to ourselves our uniquely obtained knowledge establishing that a 20-year-old man is at risk over the possibility of a blood vessel potentially bursting inside his head, when disclosure could likely save his life?

Inconceivable, right? Is there any wonder, then, that I've asked my law students to leave their moral training at the class's doorstep? But perhaps more important, one must note that society long ago, as made clear in 1998 by the U.S. Supreme Court, accepted the notion that it is critical that clients have the assurance that their lawyers will take their secrets to the grave. Nonetheless, at risk of a claim of apostasy by colleagues at the bar, one must wonder whether society is best served by a protocol that – when the rubber meets the road, as in the instances described above – risks safety and life itself in order to protect those who are in fact civilly liable or even criminally guilty.

Yes, many members of the public may believe that the duty of confidentiality imposed on lawyers by the oath they take is designed to protect *the innocent*. But, in fact, it is designed to foster a relationship between client and attorney and not necessarily to promote justice. Just look at Lee Wayne Hunt and Alton Logan. Honorable lawyers adhered to their oaths, and actually innocent men languished in prison because of how those lawyers (properly) acted. Try explaining the integrity of that oath to your teenager who fully believes in truth, justice, and the American Way.

CHAPTER THREE

THE MADE MAN

Jimmy "the Weasel" Fratianno

What exactly is a "made man?" And how does one become such a man? The answers to those questions were well-answered by Jimmy "the Weasel" Fratianno, who was a member of the Family (with a capital "F").

First, though, a little background. *La Cosa Nostra* ("our thing") – think, *The Godfather* or *Goodfellas* or *The Sopranos*. The Italian-American criminal organization (also commonly known as the "Mafia"), has been in the United States since the late 19th century. The Italian Mafia is certainly not the only organized crime syndicate in the United States, but it was – in its heyday – the most known and notorious (its influence has waned in the last 30 years due largely to the widening of membership, which led to more members who broke their pledge and became witnesses or informants). Members of *La Cosa Nostra* have been accused of a long list of crimes, everything from racketeering to murder to narcotics trafficking to gambling to prostitution to loan-sharking – and with the very plain goal, virtually always, of making money.

Back in the 1940s, one did not easily become a made member of *La Cosa Nostra*. A prospective member had to be proposed; the boss of the Family had to agree. Sometimes the Family would demand that the proposed member do something significant, literally kill someone, to prove his worthiness. Once vetted and approved, there is an initiation ceremony – the oath, if you will. Fratianno, the first person to do so in an American courtroom, publicly explained in testimony what occurred when he became "made" in 1947:

Q: What kinds of persons are allowed to become members of *La Cosa Nostra?*

A: Well, you have to be Italian.

Q: Who decides if a person can become a member of *La Cosa Nostra?*

A: Well, number one, you've got to be proposed [by a member]. The boss decides if you're to become a member, the boss of the Family . . . Sometimes you have to do something significant, like kill somebody . . . to prove you're the right person to get in.

Q: Now, when a person becomes a member of *La Cosa Nostra*, what if any, initiation ceremony is carried out?

A: Well, I can tell you about the one that I attended and they're all more or less the same. Some vary. Some have big dinners. You know, just variations. But the basics are all the same.

When I got initiated it was late forty-seven or early forty-eight. There was five of us. They brought me in first. I think at the time we had fifty to sixty members, and maybe forty to forty-five were present. They had a long table. The boss and underboss would sit on one side; the *capos* [made men who headed crews] on the end. There was a gun and a sword in the middle of the table crossing each other.

The boss would . . . we would all stand up. We would hold our hands together and the boss would rattle something off in Sicilian. That would take maybe two or three minutes.

After that they would prick your finger with a sword or with a pin to draw blood. And they would take you around to each member, introduce you and you kiss them on the cheek. That's the initiation.

Q: What, if anything, had you done to qualify for membership?

A: Well, the time I got made, I don't know if I did anything significant but I know a few months later I did something.

Q: Was that a murder . . . ?

A: Yes.

Q: You used the phrase just a moment ago, "made." What does that mean?

A: Well, you're a "made guy." That means you're a member of the organization.

Q: In what city were you initiated?

A: Los Angeles, California . . . a winery on Western Boulevard.

Q: How is it possible to resign from *La Cosa Nostra*?

A: You can't resign. You go in alive and go out dead.

Q: Is that a rule?

A: That's the law.

Q: What, if any, other rules are there that are imposed on members of *La Cosa Nostra?*

And this is where we learned about the moral code, of sorts, of *La Cosa Nostra:*

> I was told that you couldn't deal in narcotics; you could never talk to an FBI agent; you could never talk to any officers of any kind; you can't go on a grand jury and tell the truth; you can't testify in no way. You can't fool around with anybody's family. They say that the Family comes first. If your wife is dying and they need you for something, you have to leave her. These are things they tell you when you're initiated.

Finally, Fratianno told the world about the sacred oath of *omertà*– silence:

> Q: If membership in the family is secret . . . [i]s there a special way in which made guys, as you put it, are introduced to one another?
>
> A: Yes . . . well, like when they take me to introduce me to somebody they say, "Jimmy, I want you to meet so-and-so; he is a friend of ours," *amico nostra.* When they say "a friend of ours" that means a made guy.

Fratianno, a made man, kept his oath to the Family for 25 years. But when he violated that oath, he spoke to the FBI, testified against the Family, and helped send some 37 men to prison.

Jimmy Fratianno was born in Naples, Italy, in 1913, and was brought to Cleveland's Little Italy as a baby. He was introduced to crime when, at age six, he and his mother saw three men gunned down in front of a local speakeasy. She was horrified but Jimmy wasn't frightened; if anything, he was fascinated.

Fratianno's entry into the criminal world started small – but the nickname he received, "Weasel," stuck throughout his life. It was a fairly regular occurrence – little Jimmy stole fruit from the local grocer; the police saw him; he ran; the police chased him. One day, Jimmy threw a tomato at the cop before he took off. A bystander snickered: "Look at that weasel run." When writing his report, the police officer included "weasel" so that the nickname now was part of Fratianno's official record. Jimmy "the Weasel" was born.

A bartender and bootlegger at a speakeasy by age 12, Fratianno met a notorious gambler who taught him to cheat at poker and craps. Fratianno excelled and by age 14, he was fully ensconced – he marked cards, palmed loaded dice, made book and robbed as the need arose. But those activities were truly trivial when weighed against the killer Fratianno would become.

Fratianno quickly learned that he was unafraid of violence. He was an expert, and fast, ice skater. When he was 19, he showed off to impress a girl at the ice rink. Her five male friends – strangers to Fratianno – were not so impressed and brutally beat Fratianno for having shown off. Fratianno's nose had to be reconstructed with skin and cartilage from his chest.

Fratianno was less concerned with the recommended plastic surgery than he was with revenge. Over the next year, Fratianno and a friend methodically and ploddingly looked for each of the five boys who put him in the hospital. One by one, while each was alone, Fratianno and his friend mercilessly beat the four that they found, each to within an inch of his life. The fifth managed to run and was never found. Jimmy searched, but ultimately decided four out of five was enough.

A year or so later, a local district leader came to Fratianno with a scheme to cheat the government using Fratianno's father's trucking business. Unlike Fratianno, his father didn't want to be involved in anything crooked, so Fratianno leased his own trucks and made his own money. He was often at the Italian-American clubhouse – a hangout for the local bigshots. Motivated almost exclusively by the goal of making money, Fratianno began a limo service, and those at the clubhouse were a great source of business. Fratianno was living a sweet life. He was also becoming known to "The Combination" – Cleveland's Jewish-Italian mob, with which he worked for years to come.

Unions were trying to break into the garage business – Fratianno destroyed cars and busted heads, thus helping to convince garage owners to unionize. By 1935, he joined leaders of The Combination when it opened its first casino in Florida. He made book at Hialeah for such notables as Lucky Luciano (then under criminal investigation) and his crew. Back in Cleveland, Fratianno and his friends decided it was more profitable to rob gambling joints than to run crooked games. One robbery landed him in jail, where he met other mobsters. Just before Fratianno was released, he spoke of heading to the West Coast. One of the men he met in jail suggested Fratianno look up one Johnny Roselli, when he got to Los Angeles.

Roselli, behind the scenes, headed the Los Angeles Family. After proving himself to Roselli, in 1947, Fratianno was "made" in that solemn ceremony and was later promoted to *caporegime* – captain of his own crew. Fratianno did what he needed to do for the Family. He was involved in six murders; and personally committed five others. And he murdered for, what the Family (and perhaps Fratianno) believed were good reasons: the "Two Tonys" robbed a hotel in which the Family had an interest; Louie Strauss was attempting to extort a friend; Frank Niccoli refused to leave his mob boss and work with the Los Angeles Family; Anthony Brancato was stealing without the sanction of the Family; and so on.

Fratianno became disenchanted with the Los Angeles Family, after the death of its boss. With Roselli's blessing, Fratianno joined the Chicago Family. Yet, Fratianno wanted to be in Vegas – he wanted to own a casino. But he was stopped at every turn – the Gambling Commission shut him down. Fast forward to the late 1960s, early 1970s. The FBI now had in place an Organized Crime Strike Force, dedicated to stopping Mafia activity. At the same time, Fratianno found himself back in prison for fraud. The FBI pursued him for information, both in prison and out. At one point, prior to a court appearance, the prison transferred Fratianno from his assigned prison to one in which he spent eight days in solitary – in a windowless, unheated cell. He complained to the judge, who all but dismissed his complaint, but ordered that Fratianno be returned to his original jail. Upon arriving, Fratianno learned that his sentence of "one-to-three years," was actually three years with no chance of parole. Was this the FBI's doing? It is not clear. But there is no question that the FBI tried to turn Fratianno, a made man who had been in the Mafia, in one form or another, almost all his life. And let's face it – although Fratianno might disagree, he was not exactly a man of honor.

And so an informal arrangement developed. The FBI gave Fratianno some leeway in his activities; Fratianno gave the FBI some (often) dated information – information which he was sure the government already knew. Perhaps Fratianno would give the FBI information about a rival Family, all to the benefit of Fratianno. Also important to someone like Fratianno – the government paid him for what was often useless information. His efforts gained him some $20,000 in government money.

One may ask why the government put up with Fratianno providing useless information – and paid him for it, no less. Simply, the government was playing the long game. And in a series of events over the next two years, its gamble paid off.

In 1975, the then-boss of the Los Angeles Family was headed to prison, and the Acting Boss agreed to the position only if he and Fratianno could run the Los Angeles Family together. Fratianno accepted the "honor," but soon became suspicious that he was being set up. Fratianno learned there was a contract out on his good friend, Frank Bompensiero, and Fratianno felt he was made co-head of the Family to lure "Bomp" to his death. Fratianno stalled the contract as long as he could; Bomp was eventually shot while standing in a phone booth by a mob associate who, himself, was looking to be made.

It was closing in. Bomp was dead. Roselli, one of Fratianno's closest friends and allies, was killed by the Chicago Family; he was asphyxiated by someone holding a washcloth over his face. Another old friend disappeared in Cleveland. Fratianno had held himself out as head of the Family (not acting head) while his superior was in jail – he was now being accused of "misrepresenting himself" and disrespecting the Family. A rumor had been started that Fratianno went rogue and was running a separate crew and trying to take control of the West Coast. Fratianno was the target of several FBI investigations. Indeed, Fratianno recognized that in his discussions with the FBI, it often knew more than Fratianno was willing to disclose.

Fratianno was being pursued by both the mob and the government. And then, the final straw. Fratianno went to a friend's wake in Cleveland. The Cleveland Family showed Fratianno a sheet of paper which made it clear that the mob had a list of the FBI's confidential informants. Among others, Bomp was on that list.

Fratianno asked Cleveland to get more information about West Coast informants, but the reality was that he was terrified that he would be on that list. No one would understand that Fratianno gave the FBI inconsequential information; no one would care that he did it for the money – no, Fratianno was a rat and if found out, he would be brutally murdered. There really was no doubt. And so Fratianno did the only thing he could – he called the FBI and told them everything.

Everything a made man for 25 years had to tell. And at the end of the day, he was one of the most valuable informants the FBI ever had, shining a light on *La Cosa Nostra* and helping to send some 37 men to prison.

Fratianno did not abide by his oath, but he would say it was the Family – not he – that broke the rules: "Everytime I go into a courtroom, my stomach turns a little. I'm betraying a trust. *Omertà*, the silence. But all I did all my life was give away money and kill for those dirty c**su**ers. Well, sure I'm betraying a trust, but they forced me, by trying to clip me."

DISCUSSION

"Mafia" – even though it is a term not used by the initiated, what does it really mean? According to one source, the word derives, backwards, from "*afam*," which in dialect means "hunger" – which status leads one to seek to survive at any cost and by any means. It flowed from Sicily's ability to withstand the foreign powers and the "Italian boot" that was put on the "Sicilian neck." Historically, Sicily's conquerors had depleted its natural resources and Sicilians came to look upon poverty as a constant. They would do anything to escape it, and fought with neighbors who may have had more, or taken more, almost akin to stories of America's old west. And from this mindset came *La Cosa Nostra* and utter devotion to one's "Family." With that backdrop, we discuss the oath and honor code of the Mafia's "made men."

We mention the eleven murders Fratianno participated in and committed ever so casually, using the same almost-soft tone Fratianno would typically use when he spoke, as he did with me in April, 1980. He sat that Friday morning in my Justice Department Organized Crime Strike Force office preparing for his grand jury appearance that morning. Just imagine sitting across an office desk from a man calmly telling you whom he killed, and precisely when, why, and how. The one most memorable was his description of garroting a deserving "victim" with a thick rope around the victim's neck, re-counting the incident using a rope he saw lying on my desk that had wrapped a package I had coincidentally received that morning.

Unlike the other oaths described in this volume, Fratianno's oath – that of a Mafioso – was taken by a thief and a murderer. Thus, even if his murder victims may have richly deserved their violent deaths, Fratianno and his confederates wouldn't have been able to justify their killings as the actions of men of honor in a non-Mafia society. To the uninitiated, those acts were murders, pure and simple. They were totally antithetical to any other concept of honor or morality. But to the mob, they were presumably sanctioned and justified deaths.

I didn't ask Fratianno that morning if he thought that he somehow acted honorably in committing those murders. That was not the point. We had created a bond in the form of a symbiotic relationship between us for a very limited purpose: he needed me to help confirm his compliance with his obligation as a "cooperator" with the Justice Department in order to remain in the Witness Protection Program; and I needed his "singular" (meaning, otherwise unavailable) testimony about a high-ranking Mafioso whom I was seeking to prosecute. (As an aside, the Mafioso I sought to indict turned out, himself, to be a supposedly invaluable FBI informant, a fact unknown at the time to me and my team. The FBI prevailed on us to forego the prosecution.)

But as to Fratianno, the question of whether he felt the least bit of moral compunction in having been a stone murderer was irrelevant. Although one might question my own cavalier imperviousness to having made a deal with a murderer, the question of honor or morality was irrelevant to both of us. Still, one might ask, how could men like Fratianno see honor in the particular oath he took? To me, he was a murderous thug. But in his world, at least until he started talking, he worked within the confines of a moral code. And when Fratianno did speak about his years as a made man and his Mafia-oath-based conduct, he did so in a very matter-of-fact, almost business-is-business way, which actually helped the FBI convict so many mobsters.

Joe Valachi, a notorious "rat" (or "flipper," as might say President Trump), had broken his oath of *omertà* more than a decade before Fratianno did, but Valachi testified briefly in only one trial where his testimony was of marginal value. Yet Valachi's testimony did something extremely important – he confirmed that *La Cosa Nostra* was in the U.S., and that it was a real organization, putting to rest the "myth" theretofore perpetuated by FBI Director J. Edgar Hoover that the Mafia simply did not exist at all.

For his part, Fratianno enjoyed the life and "the lifestyle" – it may have reached its apex by his encounter with Frank Sinatra (about whom he testified in the government's effort to actually establish Sinatra as mob-connected). But, it appears, Fratianno knew exactly who he was. He took a blood oath and was obliged to abide by it at penalty of death ("You go in alive and go out dead").

He offered no hint that in taking up arms with the Justice Department he sought to "repent" from his past. Those like Fratianno, indeed most of them, break their oath and join "Team USA" only to avoid a lifetime in jail, or death at the hands of the Mafia itself.

Other Mafioso, though, look at their oath differently. Valachi, for example, wrote to his biographer Peter Maas, saying this:

Naturally if I could do my life over again, I would. Who would not? Now I am alone in this world. As you know, I do not write to my wife and my son as they will have nothing to do with me and I don't blame them.

Vito Genovese [boss of one of New York's five crime families] is responsible for everything. The boys brought him all these stories about

> me and he believed them. But when he was scheming against me, I was
> scheming back. ***

> I hope the American people will benefit by knowing what the mob is
> like. If I was killed in Atlanta [Penitentiary], I would have died branded
> as a rat anyway without doing anything wrong. So what did I lose?

It seems Valachi would have been branded a "rat" regardless of whether he spoke to the FBI. But was Valachi sorry, and if so, for what – being a member of the Mafia? Speaking to the FBI? We don't really know why he broke his oath, but let's look at it. Does it matter if he did so for his very survival (literally)? Or can one look at the oath and be so appalled by it and the Family régime that one would believe violating the oath was, in fact, the honorable thing to do no matter the reason?

There is another "rat" worth mentioning. The late Joseph Bonanno was one of the original five crime Family bosses of New York. He wrote an autobiography, *A Man Of Honor*. Think about that – the head of a Family wrote an autobiography. To put it in perspective, Bonanno was the one who decided whether others had sufficiently proven themselves to take the oath – and the oath they took was essentially to serve him as head of the Family.

Bonanno speaks about the Mafia as a "Family" in the more traditional sense of the word and reflects upon those he helped. Yes, Bonanno likely did some good deeds and helped some people. (John Gotti, the notorious Gambino Family boss, also likely believed he did good deeds by keeping street crime out of Howard Beach in ways the police could not). Bonanno's description of his life seems to idealize and ennoble his life in the mob:

> I have tried to be a good Father. I have helped many people. No man
> can say I cheated him or took away what was rightly his. . . I've had to

protect myself and my people, but I've never been bloodthirsty. . . I've remained true to my name and scrupulous to my principles.

***

Mafia is a form of clan cooperation to which its individual members pledge lifelong loyalty. In other words, as corny or as simple as it may sound, what makes the process work is we believe in *friendship.*

Friendship, connections, family ties, trust, loyalty, obedience – this was the "glue" that held us together.

***

In any case, what Americans call "Mafia" never was an institution, an organization, a corporate body.

***

I consider myself luckier than the generation of today in America. I was born into a Tradition. I was born among a people whom experience had taught to cherish certain fixed values. This Tradition was the flower of our culture. It taught us right and wrong. It guided youngsters as they strove toward manhood. It guided mature men, and punished them if they deserved it. Our Tradition gave us a way of life.

***

I have learned that true power comes from self-control.

I have learned that true strength comes from a clear conscience.

I have learned that true wealth comes from a good family and good friends.

This chapter challenges the reader to better understand the meaning of an oath when taken by a cold-blooded murderer. Assuming Bonanno actually believed what he was saying here, did he horribly mislead himself? Did he rationalize his actions? Or, perhaps, did he truly believe his good deeds outweighed his criminal acts?

While miscreants may indeed possess redeeming characteristics – for example, feeding the poor, or treating animals with kindness – it is hardly their oath that creates that nobility. Bonanno broke his oath in order to somehow recreate himself. Fratianno and Valachi broke their oaths to protect themselves. Is there any nobility or even true meaning in such an oath?

***

Afterthought: A colleague challenges my "unnuanced" view of the "code of honor" Bonanno purportedly embraced, which presents a supposedly honorable life, even though he was a crime Family boss. The critique reminds me of a short essay by a Yale undergraduate published in *Time* magazine shortly after 9/11. She had attended her regularly scheduled class on September 12, 2001, at which her professor proposed that the students consider the actions of the hijackers from their point of view. The student's thoughtful essay explained that, sometimes, and about some things, there is simply no nuance or "other side."

CHAPTER FOUR

THE CONSCIENTIOUS OBJECTOR

Muhammad Ali, previously known as Cassius Clay (SN)

THE OATH

We've all heard the story – the great heavyweight boxer, Muhammad Ali, was stripped of his title and the right to fight in the ring during much of his prime, when he refused induction into the Army during the Vietnam War. But how did it really come about? And what oaths did Ali take, and refuse to take, that led to his exoneration in the U.S. Supreme Court?

Conscription – also known as the draft – was in place from 1940 until 1973, when the draft was abrogated in the wake of Vietnam. In short, the draft required that all male U.S. citizens between the ages of 18 and 26 register with the Selective Service System so that there would be enough troops if the armed forces couldn't fill its ranks with volunteers. If called upon – if drafted – a person would be required to serve, and take a soldier's oath:

> I do solemnly swear (or affirm) that I will support and defend the
> Constitution of the United States and the State of (STATE NAME)
> against all enemies, foreign and domestic; that I will bear true faith and
> allegiance to the same; and that I will obey the orders of the President
> of the United States and the Governor of (STATE NAME) and the

orders of the officers appointed over me, according to law and regulations. So help me God.

By 1964, there were more than 23,000 U.S. troops in Vietnam and the draft was well in place. At that time, most Americans still believed in the war – invoking the term "domino theory." That concept allowed that if North Vietnam prevailed, communism would infect Asia and other non-communist societies would fall, like dominoes. Not until somewhat later did America became relentlessly divided about whether the U.S. should be involved in what was, in reality, a civil war taking place halfway across the world in a place that most Americans couldn't even identify on a map.

1964 was also the year that Cassius Clay – as he was then known – became the heavyweight boxing champion of the world (that is, for the first time). It was also when he announced that he had joined the Nation of Islam (led by the Honorable Elijah Muhammad) and would thereafter be known as Muhammad Ali. In doing so, Ali agreed to be bound by the teachings of the Holy Qur'an, as understood through the teachings of Elijah Muhammad. As the U.S. Supreme Court would explain years later, the Qur'an teaches that a believer shall participate only in a "just war," a religious war ("jihad") called for by Allah against non-believers.

The Nation of Islam tells us:

> We have always been taught to respect the laws of the land. We are
> taught never to carry arms, to make war or to be the aggressor, for this
> is against the nature of the righteous. We are taught the Principles of
> Divine Unity and the Universal Brotherhood of Islam.

Based on these teachings, when Ali was drafted in 1966 (and the war was beginning to reach its apex), he asked to be able to serve as a conscientious objector, i.e., one who is assigned to alternate service which would have allowed him to make a "meaningful contribution" in a non-combative capacity, through working, for example, in education or health care. But the Selective Service would not grant that request and when Ali was called to serve, he refused to take the soldier's oath. To grant conscientious objector status to an individual capable of "killing" another person with his fists, and whose religion allowed him to believe in war – just not this war – seemed, at the time, problematic, not only to the draft board, but to perhaps an overwhelming majority of white Americans as well. Particularly given that the religion itself specifically justified and encouraged jihad.

How does – or more directly, how did – the oath of a soldier and adherence to the tenets of the Nation of Islam conflict? And how did Ali, the courts, and the citizenry of the United States, choose to deal with Ali's conflict?

THE STORY

Cassius Clay – Muhammad Ali – "the Greatest." He was a leading force in boxing through the 1960s and 1970s. He remains toward the top of just about every list of the greatest athletes of all time. As a boxer, he didn't just claim to "float like a butterfly, sting like a bee," he actually did. He had speed, agility, grace, and style, all unusual for a heavyweight. Not to mention a silver tongue – Ali's taunts and pronouncements are legendary, but were extremely provocative at the time.

Having won the gold medal in the 1960 Olympics, Clay turned professional and quickly rose to fame. By 1964, he had an opportunity to fight Sonny Liston, who himself had become the heavyweight champion when he knocked out the reigning, and formidable, Floyd Patterson in the first round. Clay thus entered the Liston fight as the underdog. Liston was a tough competitor. But as Clay and Liston fought, and the seventh round was about to begin, Liston spit out his mouth guard. He had taken a beating in the sixth round, and whether it was Liston or his corner that called the fight – we don't know. But what we do know is that Clay danced around the ring, arms raised in victory, yelling "I'm the greatest! I shook up the world!"

And with that win, Clay became the heavyweight champion of the world at the age of 22. Days later, Clay announced that he would no longer be known by his "slave name," Clay; that he was now and for-ever Muhammad Ali. He had been studying with Elijah Muhammad and converted from Christianity to become a member of the Nation of Islam, where he later became a minister.

Controversy immediately engulfed Ali (even with his own father). The Nation of Islam, whose members are also known as "Black Muslims," was (and remains) an extremely controversial religion. It has had many followers, Malcolm X and Louis Farrakhan perhaps the most visible, and has suffered its own internal conflicts over the decades. The Nation of Islam, at the time of Elijah Muhammad (and Ali), stood for principles which Elijah Muhammad set out in *Message to the Blackman in America*. These principles often pitted white and black against one another. Ali saw the Nation as embracing; many white people saw it as a radical sect with a separatist, and even criminal, agenda. But Ali – ever the great athlete and provocateur – seemed to rise above it all.

In 1966, with the U.S. now in the thick of the Vietnam War, Ali received notice that he had been drafted by his Selective Service board. He formally requested the right to serve as a conscientious objector based on his religious objection to a war between non-believers. His request was reviewed by the authorities, yet denied. Ali had a choice – he could report for duty and challenge his designation while he served in the armed forces, or he could refuse to serve and risk criminal pros-ecution. Ali chose the latter, and in what became a media event, Ali reported to the induction center, yet refused to literally "step forward" when they called his name.

In May 1967, Ali was indicted by a federal grand jury for failing to submit to induction. His trial began a month later and lasted two days. It was a spectacle, to be sure, given his place in American society. Ali argued he was a minister of the Nation of Islam, that his religion did not believe in the war, and that he should therefore not be required to serve. The (all white) jury deliberated for all of 20 minutes before finding him guilty. He was sentenced to the maximum penalty of five years, and a $10,000 fine. The judge, however, allowed Ali to remain free while he appealed the decision.

Immediately upon the guilty verdict, the New York State Athletic Commission revoked Ali's license. Other states promptly followed suit. And when Ali sought to fight in Japan, the U.S. government objected, and Ali was required to surrender his passport. At the age of 25, the heavyweight champion of the world was benched, and his boxing title was revoked.

Ali, a fighter after all, fought through the courts. By the time he got to the Supreme Court, Americans' view of the war had changed dramatically. No longer were people in fear of the Communist threat, or at least no longer felt that an incursion half-way across the world was justified or justifiable. By November 1967, close to 500,000 Americans were in Vietnam; the war was brought to our living rooms in ways no other war was or could have been. "Our boys" were coming home addicted to drugs, suffering from what we now call post-traumatic stress disorder (PTSD), or what we now know to be the side effects of Agent Orange. And with this, Ali became more than just Ali – he was a symbol for all that was wrong with America's engagement in Vietnam.

His case – perhaps due to who he was – made it to the U.S. Supreme Court in 1971. By the time the Court heard the case, the government had largely conceded that Ali's objections to fighting in the Vietnam War were sincere and based on his religious training and belief – both of which were sufficient to have allowed him to have conscientious objector status. As a result, the Court was able to reverse Ali's conviction on largely procedural grounds, with one judge's concurrence discussing the Qur'an's teachings on "unjust" wars. Even so, when one reads the decision, one feels that the judges took great liberties with talmudic-like nuance to get to the result they wanted – generally not what one thinks of when thinking about decisions made by our highest court.

One year before the Supreme Court decision, a federal district court in New York decided that the Athletic Commission had overstepped its authority. Ali could fight again! And so, after 43 months in exile, Ali returned to the ring. It took him four years, but he regained the heavy-weight title, beating George Forman in the "Rumble in the Jungle" in Zaire. He lost the title four years later to Leon Spinks, only to regain it in a rematch seven months later. Ali retired from boxing at age 39, with a record of 56 wins, 5 losses.

For those who observed the decline in Ali's physical and mental status over the years, one wonders whether, if his religious beliefs had forbidden him from engaging in violence of any sort, Ali would have lived longer with a better quality of life. Or perhaps the pugilist's "oath to himself" as a fighter – like that of a matador bound to perform in the *anillo de toros* – although not articulated nor recognized formally, insisted that Ali continue fighting in the ring as long as the strength in his body allowed him to.

DISCUSSION

There seems to be no "oath" that an individual takes when he or she converts to Christianity, Judaism, or Islam – the three principal mono-theistic religions of the world. Yes, one is obliged in each instance to reject other deities; but at the exquisite moment of undertaking that religion "new" to the converted individual, there is surely no oath that forbids violence or war, other than perhaps the oath to be bound by the tenets of one's chosen religion. In Islam, or the Nation of Islam, ironically to some, followers must not engage in a war unless directed by Allah, and then only in the instance of a war against the "infidel."

In retrospect, contemporary thinking tells us that the Vietnam War was deplorable in so many respects. And there were many "draft dodgers" – people who did not step forward simply because they thought the war was wrong or not worth the personal risk; not because of their religious vows, but because of their political beliefs or risk to personal safety. Some hid in the U.S. or found some kind of draft deferments such as bone spurs; many made new homes in Canada – actually leaving their country to avoid a war. Many never returned to the U.S., even after President Jimmy Carter, on his second day of office in 1977, pardoned all Vietnam War draft evaders.

But at the time that Ali fought, his participation in active fighting in Vietnam (which may have never even come about – he would likely have been assigned to serve elsewhere as an entertainer of sorts, one supposes), the government had issues with Ali's refusal to participate. Many non-adherents may ask how the religion can allow a holy war but forbid a secular war, even if the government of their country, rightly or wrongly, finds the war in the interests of national security, as was ostensibly the case with Vietnam.

And so Muhammad Ali basically asked the Supreme Court to retroactively authorize him to have abstained from actual fighting in a war that "his religious oath" – even if he didn't technically take an oath – forbade his participation in. So, let's put aside that Ali made his living through engaging in violent behavior, the question asked was whether there is a religious hypocrisy in a willingness to do battle in one type of war, yet not another. And further, has the law, if unintentionally, created a conflict that elevates religious oath over secular obligation? Meaning Cassius Clay had to go to war, whereas Muhammad Ali didn't.

In the wake of *Clay v. United States*, assuming a draft were reinstated, can an unprincipled agnostic or atheist pretend adherence to the religious principles of Islam in order to avoid fighting? They could try. But *Clay* does tell us that believers in Islam should not be required to fight a war not sanctioned by their religion. Which makes us wonder how to reconcile that so many Muslims – surely many observant among them – willingly and voluntarily serve in the American military, including in Afghanistan or Iraq. Those are not holy wars, nor is American involvement seemingly consistent with the tenets of Islam.

What makes an "oath" part of the Ali story is his refusal to take the only real oath that was implicated – the obligation by every eligible American male to take the soldier's oath. Does that mean Ali was a bad citizen, or that he didn't have to take the soldier's oath because of his religious beliefs?

So, was it the soldier's oath or his religious belief that should have prevailed?

CHAPTER FIVE

THE PHYSICIAN

Dr. Samuel A. Mudd

THE OATH

It is said that the Greek physician, Hippocrates (c. 460 – 380 B.C.E.), is the "Father of Medicine." His lasting contributions, however, far exceed mere treatment of the sick. He created what we now call the Hippocratic Oath, the first known memorialization of ethical rules to which doctors, healers, would adhere. Even today, as they graduate from medical school, doctors swear by the Hippocratic Oath (in original or modern form) or take the similar Oath of Maimonides (c. 1135 – 1204), renowned rabbi, physician, and philosopher.

Summed up in a soundbite, doctors promise: "First do no harm." But the oath says far more than that. As may be applicable to the story we are about to tell, those who take the oath promise:

> I will use treatment to help the sick according to my ability and judgment, but never with a view to injury and wrong-doing. *** Into whatsoever houses I enter, I will enter to help the sick, and I will abstain from all intentional wrong-doing and harm, especially from abusing the bodies of man or woman, bond or free.

Or, as Maimonides puts it:

May I never see in the patient anything but a fellow creature in pain.
*** Oh, God, Thou has appointed me to watch over the life and death of
Thy creatures; here am I ready for my vocation and now I turn unto my
calling.

Finally, there is another section of the oath pertinent here, and that is
relevant in any discussion of law and medical ethics that takes place
today, some 2,400 years after it was written:

whatsoever I shall see or hear in the course of my profession, as well as
outside my profession in my intercourse with men, if it be what should
not be published abroad, I will never divulge, holding such things to be
holy secrets.

How sacrosanct is this oath? Does it require a doctor to tend to those
who are reprehensible – to both him and society? What does a doctor
do if confronted with an injured patient who has just actually murdered the president? And, if a doctor does save that patient, will the
law protect him?

THE STORY

Which brings us to Dr. Samuel A. Mudd. Let's set the stage, as it were.
On April 9, 1865, in what would later be seen as the "official" end to
the Civil War, General Robert E. Lee surrendered his 28,000 troops
to Union General Ulysses S. Grant at Appomattox, Virginia. Five days
later, on April 14 – Good Friday, in fact – President Abraham Lincoln
and his wife kept their appointment to see the play *Our American
Cousin* at Ford's Theater in Washington, D.C. During the second act,
a well-known actor of the day, John Wilkes Booth, opened the door to

Lincoln's box and fatally shot Lincoln. Major Henry Rathbone, a guest of the Lincolns, immediately tried to detain Booth who, pulling a knife, was able to escape by jumping from the box to the stage. In doing so, he broke the fibula above the ankle in his left leg.

This murder, though, was part of a larger plot. Initially, Booth's plan was to kidnap Lincoln, and hold him until certain Confederate soldiers were released from prison. But by April 14, Booth and his confreres had hatched quite a different scheme – Booth would assassinate Lincoln, while others would kill, at roughly the same time, Vice President Andrew Johnson and Secretary of State William Seward. Booth, however, was the only one who succeeded – Johnson's assigned attacker did not go through with it, and Seward survived his attack.

Now, there are varying accounts of what happened over the next days; however, let's assume the following. Dr. Mudd was a doctor and tobacco farmer in southern Maryland, some 30 miles from the Ford Theater. He was a staunch supporter of slavery – indeed, to him it was a God-given institution, and his tobacco business was affected when Maryland outlawed the practice just a year earlier. When the injured Booth showed up on Mudd's doorstep at 4:00 a.m. with another man, Mudd did what doctors do: he set Booth's leg and gave him crutches.

But Mudd did more – he gave the men a place to sleep, he gave them food and he traveled with Booth's friend into town. Now, there is little question that Mudd and Booth – both known for their pro-slavery views – had met previously and that Booth had once stayed overnight in Mudd's home. However, Mudd claimed that, on the night of the President's assassination, he never recognized Booth. Mudd claimed that when Booth and his friend arrived at Mudd's home, the men introduced themselves as Henson (David Herold) and Tyson (Booth).

Booth had long chin whiskers (Mudd's wife later thought this was a disguise) and a moustache, which he didn't have in their prior meetings. Booth covered his face in the darkness and in a shawl. Mudd, also, didn't learn of Lincoln's murder until he and Henson went into town the next day, where he and Henson separated and returned to Mudd's home separately. By the time Mudd returned to his home, Henson and Tyson were on their horses, ready to leave. In at least one account, Mudd actually told them which way to ride, in order to avoid the authorities already on their trail. No matter whether Mudd intentionally helped Booth, Booth was killed by a Union soldier 12 days after Lincoln's assassination when he was cornered but refused to surrender.

But back to Mudd. Mudd spoke to his cousin about his visitors the day after Booth left. Mudd was subsequently questioned by the authorities and, along with seven others (all told, seven men and one woman), tried by a military court – the Nuremberg Trial of its day. Mudd was convicted of conspiracy to murder the president. He escaped the death penalty by a single vote and was sentenced to life at hard labor. Throughout, among his defense claims was that he did what the Hippocratic Oath required – he helped the sick. Once imprisoned, Mudd wrote:

> Deprived of liberty, banished from home, family and friends, bound
> in chains for having exercised a simple act of common humanity in
> setting the leg of a man for whose insane act I had no sympathy, but
> which was in line with my professional calling. It was but natural that
> resentment and fear should rankle in my heart.

Setting Booth's leg was not the end of Mudd's commitment to the oath. While Mudd was later serving his sentence at Fort Jefferson, west of Key West, there was an outbreak of yellow fever. When the prison's medical officer died from the fever, Mudd, once again, did what the Hippocratic Oath required – he took over the prison hospital and tended to the sick – his captors, his fellow prisoners, whoever was in need.

Because of Mudd's actions, the death toll at Fort Jefferson was comparatively low. A survivor believed that Mudd deserved clemency, and petitioned President Andrew Johnson: "He inspired the hopeless with courage, and by his constant presence in the midst of danger and infection, regardless of his own life, tranquillized the fearful and desponding. Many here who have experienced his kind and judicious treatment can never repay him." Almost three hundred guards and prisoners signed the letter.

Mudd was pardoned in 1869. Johnson wrote that he had spoken with members of the medical profession who explained the oath Mudd had taken:

> the circumstances of the surgical aid to the escaping assassin [Booth] ... are deserving of a lenient construction as within the obligations of professional duty, and thus inadequate evidence of a guilty sympathy with the crime or the criminal.

DISCUSSION

Thinking as a layman, who lacks the commitment – or is it sensitivity? – to the oath that a physician might have, the immediate question in assessing Mudd's behavior, indeed, in judging him, is whether he knew it was Booth and what Booth had done when he arrived at Mudd's door step.

To look at it from the standards embodied in the oath, it shouldn't matter: Hippocrates and Maimonides both required that a physician's obligation to heal the sick is absolute. This, no matter how egregious the patient's conduct; indeed, even if the patient's conduct actually caused his own injury, as in Booth's case. Let's think about it in today's climate – doctors heal violent criminals; and doctors heal terrorists, even those with whom they (or their countries) are at war. Israeli doctors famously attend to Palestinian terrorists. However much a doctor viscerally despises his patients, he heals. That is what their oath requires.

Mudd, it appears, albeit from a factual record which may have been partly lost over time, was unquestionably a sympathizer in the institution of slavery, and in the Confederacy itself. Maybe the military tribunal was correct and Mudd was a co-conspirator. Does that, should that, matter in terms of Mudd's decision to treat Booth's leg?

Assuming Mudd knew it was Booth, and what Booth had done, did the oath preclude him from alerting the *gens d'armes* that Booth had been to his home and in which direction he was absconding? Does the confidentiality a physician must afford his patient allow Mudd to heal – and also shout for the authorities? And does one answer that question by relying solely on the oath, or based on today's standards where the law and the American Medical Association's Principles of Medical Ethics have pinpointed areas where confidentiality is not required, even not allowed?

Put aside the law and AMA. And put aside whether Mudd supported slavery. Suppose, as some do, that as Booth arrived at Mudd's home, Mudd knew that Booth indeed perpetrated the greatest crime in American history – a president's assassination. And creating here an anachronism– telephones would not exist for at least another 11 years – suppose that when Mudd saw Booth hobbling down the road in his direction he called the police to alert them that the person who was about to arrive was the assassin. Would such an act have violated that sacred oath? Would it have been consistent with his ethical obligations if he had delayed treating his patient to allow the police sufficient time to arrive?

Bringing it closer to home, imagine if one of the 9/11 hijackers miraculously survived the crash of the World Trade Center and was found at its base writhing in excruciating pain. Most civilians would simply pass him by and urge first responders to "just let him die." The military, of course, might want to keep him alive and even help resuscitate him hoping that he could inform on the rest of the conspiracy and its leaders. This, not because of an obligation imposed by an ethicist's thinking. Physicians, though, whether they like it or not, are called to a higher duty – to heal even those who have caused mass destruction.

But take it a step further. Suppose that, while treating his "patient," the doctor obtains information about others involved in the hijacking or, in a Mudd variation on the hypothetical, others involved in the Lincoln assassination plot. But assume it was information necessary to heal the hijacker – information, let's say, about a substance he inhaled which the doctor knew could only have been found in one village in one country in the Middle East where the conspiracy was hatched.

Society as a whole wants that doctor to reveal that information. But what does the Hippocratic Oath require? Putting aside the legal loophole that may allow the physician to disclose, on the theory that he would be protecting others from violence, would the physician be oath-bound to maintain the confidentiality of this disclosure, notwithstanding the potential value the information might have to the world? Sometimes it is counterintuitive to the ethics of a physician that the same ethical obligation which requires him to heal may require him to remain silent when information he received could help others. Think of it in terms of confession – some probably believe (and rightly so) that their religious leader will not disclose what he is told, no matter the consequences to others. As a layperson, imagine feeling constrained to both heal a murderer and to keep your knowledge of his admission of ultimate wrongdoing to yourself, at penalty of violating your profession's ethics.

If, hypothetically and today, Booth's injury was caused by a gunshot from the police as he escaped from the Ford Theater, what is Mudd to do? His Hippocratic Oath requires him to remain silent; but (imposing today's standards on this 1865 story), his legal obligation requires him to report the gunshot wound. Hasn't the law replaced the physician's oath? And what would Hippocrates, or even Maimonides, think? They lived in far different times. The AMA did not exist, and the law had not evolved to create privilege and, importantly, exceptions to privilege.

To fairly explain, ethical duties may be far different from a freestanding legal obligation. Suppose Doctor X treats a patient for HIV, and the patient acknowledges during the course of treatment that he has had consensual, but unprotected, sexual relations with five partners, including his wife, within the past year– but has not disclosed his HIV positive status to them.

Now, of course, any thoughtful and ethical physician would want to persuade the patient that it would be appropriate for the patient – and if not the patient, the doctor herself – to advise each partner whose identity he knows, so that they may best deal with the medical crisis they may already face without knowing it. But assume that the patient says no and directs his doctor to maintain confidentiality. The facts here are far different than in Mudd's case – Mudd's disclosure of Booth's visit would hardly help to save lives, whereas Dr. X could do precisely that.

The law of every state, presumably more demanding than the Hippocratic Oath, requires the doctor to report his patient's HIV status to the Center for Disease Control, but she won't know the identity of victims except the patient's wife. Hippocrates probably never thought of this conundrum – and never thought that the "law," which might affirmatively *require* that a physician violate confidentiality, would insist upon consideration of a third party's immediate medical needs.

Of course, the Mudd case and the hypothetical 9/11 case lie at the outer contours of any discussion about the oath and the obligations that the oath might impose. When someone, as a matter of law, is obligated to do something or to refrain from doing something, the question of the individual's character is placed off to the side of the road; a physician's oath is beside the point. But adherence to the oath requires a duty far broader that what the law might compel. It is, perhaps, the place where decisions are the most difficult and questions about one's character come streaming through.

Return for a moment to Mudd. Had the police asked about how Mudd's patient came to be injured and Mudd, had he simply set Booth's leg (and not given him directions how to best escape), declined to answer even if the circumstances of the injury weren't essential to the treatment, isn't it likely that his obligations as a physician, bound by his oath, would have prevailed? Perhaps not immediately, but at least in the view of history.

CHAPTER SIX
THE PRESIDENT

Franklin Delano Roosevelt

THE OATH

The person who sits in the highest office in the most powerful country in the world takes an oath. He (or she) has a responsibility to the populace, and vows:

> I do solemnly swear (or affirm) that I will faithfully execute the office of President of the United States, and will to the best of my ability, preserve, protect, and defend the Constitution of the United States.

This is a president's contract with the American people. The oath was written by the Framers; the words come directly from the Constitution. When "faithfully execut[ing]" the office, the president puts aside his or her private interests – the only interest is that of the country. Consider that in terms of complaints about the current president. And when the president vows to "preserve, protect and defend" – that means more than simply not violating the Constitution. It means to affirmatively promote the ideals for which our Founding Fathers fought.

Curiously, although the difference is likely inconsequential, the presidential oath, unlike the congressional oath, does not also specifically swear to support and defend *the Constitution* "against all enemies foreign and domestic" – particularly interesting given the issue presented here.

Did President Franklin Delano Roosevelt actually know that the Japanese would attack Pearl Harbor and, for strategically political reasons, let it occur anyway – resulting in the loss of some 2,400 American lives and much of the navy fleet docked there? A more difficult question: did he provoke Japan's attack? Historians do not agree. The authors take no position. If one assumes that Roosevelt did know – or worse, incited the attack – what does that say about his allegiance to the oath that he took as president?

Maybe we have seen the grainy, 7-minute, black and white video. On December 8, 1941, the day following the attack, FDR gave his "Day of Infamy" speech, alerting the nation that, just the day before, the U.S. had entered into the fray that was World War II. The U.S. had been attacked by the "Empire of Japan." Japan's relations with the U.S. had been strained, but at the time of the attack the two nations were ostensibly at peace, discussing a plan which would maintain peace in the Pacific. Indeed, even after the attack, the Japanese Ambassador delivered a formal reply to a recent message from the United States – in it, Japan terminated negotiations, but nowhere did it hint that Japan would attack the U.S., or acknowledge that it would have done so by the time the U.S. received the communication. "This form of treachery shall never again endanger us," Roosevelt promised.

Imperial Japan planned and executed the attack on Pearl Harbor, Oahu, Hawaii, which was, at the time, a U.S. territory. And lest there be any doubt about Japan's intentions, American ships were also torpedoed on the waters between Honolulu and San Francisco. Japan, in coordinated strikes, also attacked Hong Kong, Guam, the Philippines and other islands throughout the Pacific. And so, on December 8, 1941, with a nearly unanimous congressional vote, the U.S. entered World War II.

To put this in perspective, in December 1941, the war in Europe was raging. Germany appeared to be winning – it successfully invaded Poland, Denmark, Norway, Belgium, Luxembourg, France, Yugoslavia and Greece. It attacked Great Britain. And Italy stood by Germany's side when it bombarded Germany's former ally, Russia. In the Pacific, Japan, the third member of the "Axis" of Germany and Italy, occupied portions of China, Vietnam, Cambodia and Laos, in addition to its continuing occupation of Korea and Taiwan.

The U.S. was sitting out the bloodshed. Circa-1940 opinion polls showed that a majority of Americans didn't want our involvement in Europe's wars. Nonetheless, FDR and the military understood that a Nazi Germany-controlled Europe would threaten the United States and America's very way of life.

As early as October 1940, Naval Intelligence issued a memo containing a startling plan: incite a Japanese attack on American soil, which would mobilize America into Europe's war. The thought was that the U.S. had the ability, and the logistics, to nullify Japanese aggressive action in the Pacific so that Japan would be unable to help Germany and Italy in their campaign in Europe. The memo suggested an 8-point course of action and concluded:

> If by these means Japan could be led to commit an overt act of war against the U.S., so much the better. At all events we had to be fully prepared to accept the threat of war.

The memo's proposals were systematically effectuated, most notably an oil embargo. Oil was a crucial import, and the majority of Japan's oil came from the U.S. By November 1941, negotiations between the U.S. and Japan were going nowhere. Roosevelt told his top advisors that the U.S. would soon be at war but wanted Japan to act first. Conscious of public perception, Roosevelt raised the question whether, if Japan attacked nations other than the U.S. and the U.S. retaliated on their behalf, would the public support him. While the cabinet unanimously believed the answer was "yes," Roosevelt was uncertain. His Army Chief of Staff then leaked to reporters that we would soon be at war, presumably attempting to ensure public support for an inevitable entry into the war.

The U.S. was also working on MAGIC, its code-breaking system. In 1940, Japan began using a cipher machine (code named "Purple") which carried Japan's diplomatic, but not military, communiqués. The U.S. was thus able to decode communications so that it understood Japan's objectives, but not the means by which it sought to achieve them. The U.S. knew there would be Japanese troop movement in China; that Japan would seize control of Vietnam from the French Vichy; and, importantly, that Japan would advance into Hawaiian waters. Indeed, the U.S. even knew that Japan would discontinue negotiations with it shortly before the Pearl Harbor attack, and one day before Roosevelt officially received Japan's communication.

Immediately after the Pearl Harbor attack, people wanted answers – did the U.S. know the attack was imminent? Should it have known? Eight congressional investigations were convened, the most substantial of which was the Joint Congressional Committee Investigation into the Pearl Harbor Disaster, convened on November 15, 1945. By then, the war was over, and Harry S. Truman was president. His administration released all relevant classified documents. The majority laid blame on Japan – the attack was planned and launched while the countries were engaged in peace negotiations. The Committee found no evidence to support charges that anyone, including Roosevelt, "provoked, incited, cajoled or coerced Japan into attacking this nation in order that a declaration of war might be easily obtained from Congress." The majority determined that "virtually everyone was surprised" by the Pearl

Harbor attack, yet officers in Washington and Hawaii "were fully conscious of the danger" and that an attack on Pearl Harbor "was at least a possibility." Hawaiian commanders were guilty of errors of judgment; not derelictions of duty.

Some historians, however, have examined the evidence and determined that Roosevelt purposefully and strategically provoked Japan to attack the U.S. Others believe that the U.S. knew the Japanese were coming yet did nothing to stop it. Finally, others conclude, as the Commission did, that the U.S. was shocked and astounded by Japan's attack on our soil.

We don't have the answer. But we posit, for purposes of this exercise: *if* Roosevelt knew and did nothing to stop the attack, did he violate his oath to "preserve, protect, and defend the Constitution"?

DISCUSSION

It's easy in the extreme to second guess a president's decision making, particularly on national security matters – especially if the decision was controversial when made. For example, the decision by Abraham Lincoln to enter the war against the South; the decision by Woodrow Wilson to enter World War I; the decision by George W. Bush (Bush II) to invade Iraq.

By contrast, the decision by FDR to ask Congress to declare our entrance into World War II against Japan wasn't controversial at all when made. Indeed, the vote in the Congress on December 8, 1941 was overwhelming: 388 to 1. Jeanette Rankin, a pacifist, was the sole vote against – and she was not only met with a chorus of hisses and boos, but was voted out of office at the next opportunity.

But whether a decision by a president is "popular" or not is not the question presented here. Rather, it is whether the president violates his oath of office to "preserve, protect, and defend the Constitution" by taking an action that seems counterintuitive to what might arguably, at least, seem a sound and appropriate course of action. Is it, for example, sound and appropriate to publicly draw a line in the sand, threatening an adversary nation with the potentiality of war when the president has absolutely no intention to go to war no matter how provocative the enemy nation might be? Is it sound and appropriate to threaten to shut the government down as a "bluff" in order to move a recalcitrant Congress to a particular policy decision consistent with the president's thinking? To bring it closer to present day (and although this is purely hypothetical), would it be sound and appropriate for a president to stand by and simply allow an attack against the World Trade Center by a terrorist organization to occur – with unequivocal intelligence that it indeed would happen – in order to persuade the American public that an all-out attack on the state sponsor of that act of terrorism was fully justified?

The last hypothetical most closely resembles what is presented in the FDR/Pearl Harbor story, assuming it actually occurred. Meaning, assume FDR, fully counselled by his national security advisors, honestly believed that entrance into World War II was unavoidable and that a quicker entrance would ultimately save American lives – even if numerous lives would be lost in the short run by virtue of a Japanese attack that was allowed to occur. Aside from the horrible optics implicated, would it be significantly different from an army general taking a "long view," and directing an attack against an enemy stronghold, fully aware that half of his soldiers would invariably be killed even if the attack were successful?

What separates the president's oath, given the action allegedly taken by FDR, from other oaths is how one may "objectively" determine whether Roosevelt violated his oath. Is it assessed by whether other presidents, similarly situated but with different strategic philosophies, would have taken the same tack in allowing the nation's military to be victimized? Would it be dependent on whether the president had strong political opposition – that is, a significant portion of the nation, or at least of the opposition party, was isolationist-leaning and wanted desperately to remain neutral in the international struggle? In other words, unlike many of the other oaths discussed, there would be no objective way to determine if a president violated his oath by willingly ignoring the attack that he well knew was imminent, thus permitting a significant segment of the nation's military to be horribly victimized, as indeed occurred at Pearl Harbor.

Given the catastrophe presented at Pearl Harbor, and assuming that Roosevelt had advance knowledge, can there be a serious argument that, indeed, FDR didn't violate his oath? One could posit that to have done otherwise – that is, to have stood prepared to victoriously fight off and defeat the Japanese attack – may have theoretically pushed the nation further into isolationism. And the president may have determined doing that would have conflicted with the security interests of the United States, especially with a Nazi Europe on the verge of knocking at our door.

What also separates a president's oath from others described in this book is the impact that it's violation might have on so many others – the president's oath impacts not only the lives of those immediately effected, but potentially the lives of the entire nation. If a lawyer, or a doctor, or a priest, violates his oath, typically only few individuals, if even that many, are harmed. A violation of the president's oath, however, impacts many – in this case, literally the world (although the president's oath obligation is only to the United States).

And yet, albeit somewhat astonishingly, many citizens would argue that the president was in fact duty bound to violate it. It is impossible to calculate at this late date, if doing so were ever possible, but a poll taken today might argue that FDR did "the right thing" by allowing the attack (assuming, of course, that "he knew"). That, in the long run, the United States was benefitted by the president keeping to himself that an attack was inevitable, despite the terrible loss of life that occurred at Pearl Harbor and the resultant need for the nation to play "catch up" for so long. It might even be the case that a poll taken on December 8, 1941, excluding the families of the fallen, might have come out the same way – that the president was correct in seeking popular support for a war that he knew needed to be fought.

What does it say, however, that a determination that a president violated his oath may rest upon the popularity of the decision he made? Or that the determination may be radically different depending on whether the determination is reached contemporaneously with the president's action that supposedly violated his oath, or is made in hindsight?

America today, aside perhaps from the civil liberties community (although maybe not all of it), is largely untroubled that Abraham Lincoln suspended the writ of habeas corpus during the Civil War, given that Lincoln fought the war as a due process proponent. This, even though large stretches of American society at the time, even in the North, strongly opposed the action that Lincoln felt the need to take. Still, history is written by the victors.

Interestingly, America, at the time, didn't condemn President Truman for dropping the atomic bomb which brought a quick end to World War II and thereby saved American lives. Whereas today many condemn the barbarity of the act, and Truman for having authorized it. Still, almost none would argue today that Truman violated his oath to protect and defend the Constitution in having dropped the bomb.

Unlike the other oaths discussed here, it does seem that popularity contests, and the current views of the body politic at a particular moment in time and at a particular geographic location within the nation, are the principal determinants of whether a president complied with or broke his oath. It remains to be seen what the nation believes on that score about our current president on November 3, 2020. Or fifty years later. Not to mention how he is perceived in the "blue" versus "red" states, respectively.

CHAPTER SEVEN
The Citizen

Fred Toyosaburo Korematsu

THE OATH

When one becomes a citizen of the United States, an oath – the Oath of Allegiance – must be taken:

> I hereby declare, on oath [solemnly affirm], that I absolutely and
> entirely renounce and abjure all allegiance and fidelity to any foreign
> prince, potentate, state, or sovereignty of whom or which I have
> heretofore been a subject or citizen; that I will support and defend
> the Constitution and laws of the United States of America against all
> enemies, foreign and domestic; that I will bear true faith and allegiance
> to the same; that I will bear arms on behalf of the United States when
> required by the law; that I will perform noncombatant service in the
> Armed Forces of the United States when required by the law; that I will
> perform work of national importance under civilian direction when
> required by the law; and that I take this obligation freely without any
> mental reservation or purpose of evasion [so help me God].

Of course, those born in the United States need not take the oath. It is presumed, rightly or wrongly, that we support and defend the Constitution and the United States without reservation. But what happens when our country tells us that, whether we were born else-where and took the citizenship oath, or born here so that the oath was unnecessary, we need to vacate our homes, leave our possessions, and be moved to an internment camp, all because our parents or ancestors were born in a country with which the U.S. was then at war?

Fred T. Korematsu embodies the iniquities of our country's response to World War II and how it treated its own citizens.

THE STORY

Fred Korematsu was born in Oakland, California, in 1919. His parents were Japanese immigrants who ran a floral nursery. After the U.S. entered WWII, Korematsu tried to enlist in the National Guard or the Coast Guard. America was his country too, and he wanted to defend it. But Korematsu was rejected – he was of Japanese ancestry and America was at war with the Japanese.

Two months after Japan bombed Pearl Harbor in Honolulu (which officially brought the U.S. into WWII), President Franklin Roosevelt signed Executive Order 9066 on February 19, 1942:

> Whereas the successful prosecution of the war requires every possible
> protection against espionage and against sabotage to national-defense
> material, national-defense premises, . . .

> Now, therefore, by virtue of the authority vested in me as President
> of the United States, and Commander in Chief of the Army and Navy,
> I hereby authorize and direct the Secretary of War, and the Military
> Commanders . . ., whenever he or any designated Commander deems
> such action necessary or desirable, to prescribe military areas in such

places and of such extent as he or the appropriate Military Commander may determine, from which any or all persons may be excluded, and ***

I hereby further authorize and direct the Secretary of War and the said Military Commanders to take such other steps as he or the appropriate Military Commander may deem advisable to enforce compliance with the restrictions applicable to each Military area ***

Remarkable. The military can make any area it deems a restricted area "from which any or all persons may be excluded." Now, the Executive Order, on its face, didn't single out those of Japanese descent, or any other group of people based on race. But it allowed for the issuance of several military proclamations and congressional orders, culminating, on May 3, 1942, in the military's Civilian Exclusion Order No. 34. After 12 o'clock on May 8, 1942, all persons of Japanese ancestry, both alien and non-alien, were to be excluded from "Military Area No. 1," which included the County of Alameda, California. The theory was that it would address the nation's fears of further Japanese attack or sabotage, particularly on the West Coast, where naval ports, commercial shipping and agriculture were most vulnerable. Or put another way, Japanese Americans would somehow be complicit if Japan attacked the mainland.

In effect, the Executive Order allowed the armed forces to remove (apparently without check) people of Japanese ancestry from their homes under threat of criminal prosecution. Ultimately, more than 120,000 people of Japanese birth, or ancestry (even if only one ancestor), were moved to detention camps. They left their homes, their pets, and any possessions which they could not carry with them. Many sold their homes and property for whatever they could, (correctly) not confident that it would be there when/if they returned. Most of the people who were relocated lived on the West Coast and two-thirds were American citizens, some third generation. Many had never even visited Japan.

To be clear, the Japanese who were subject to this exclusion order were not told – "go live with family or friends elsewhere," which would have been objectionable enough. Rather they were required to first report to a facility, where they were processed and moved to internment camps, or concentration camps as they have been called. The camps were hastily put together. They often consisted of military style barracks with 25 people living in a space designed to accommodate four. Wood stoves, poor ventilation. Shared, external bathrooms and showers, mostly unsanitary, leading to disease.

Children were schooled in "classrooms" which had few windows, so that they were sweltering with little air or ventilation. There were roughly 48 students to a teacher at the elementary school age. School supplies were a luxury. And to make sure the Japanese understood their predicament, these camps were surrounded by barbed wire with armed guards in towers.

Needless to say, when those who were "detained" were permitted to return home – by 1946, all of the camps had closed – nothing was the same. Jobs had been lost; and if they didn't sell their home before leaving, it may not have been there when they returned.

Korematsu – born here, and who tried to enlist in the military to serve his country – was 23 years old. He lived in Alameda County and refused to surrender to be placed in an internment camp. In order to avoid detection, Korematsu had minor plastic surgery to alter his eyes. He changed his name to Clyde Sarah and claimed to be of Spanish and Hawaiian descent.

All to no avail. He was arrested on May 30, 1942 and was taken to a county jail. While there, representatives of the American Civil Liberties Union came to meet with him and asked if he would be willing to be *the* test case – the ACLU wanted to challenge the constitutionality of the government's imprisonment of Japanese Americans.

Korematsu quickly agreed, but his defense was unsuccessful. He was tried and convicted in federal court for violating the military orders issued under Executive Order 9066. He was sentenced to a term of five years' probation and transported, first to a holding center in California, and ultimately to Utah, where the government had set up one of its ten camps. Korematsu appealed, and his case ultimately made it to the Supreme Court by October 1944.

At the time, there were WWII battles daily. The Japanese launched new invasions against Britain and China. U.S./Australian forces met Japanese cruisers in the Philippines for possibly the largest naval battle in history.

And with this backdrop, the *Korematsu* case was before the Supreme Court. In a 6-3 decision, it first recognized that any legal restriction on a single racial group is suspect, and thus the government would be held to a high level of scrutiny. However, the Exclusion Order, as it was known, was designed as a "protection against espionage and against sabotage" and thus within the "war power" of the government. The majority of the justices found that:

> Korematsu was not excluded . . . because of hostility to him or his race. He was excluded because we are at war with the Japanese Empire because the properly constituted military authorities feared an invasion of our West Coast and felt constrained to take proper security measures, because they decided that the military urgency of the situation demanded that all citizens of Japanese ancestry be segregated from the West Coast temporarily, and, finally, because Congress, reposing its confidence in this time of war in our military leaders – as inevitably it must – determined that they should have the power to do just this. There was evidence of disloyalty on the part of some, the military authorities considered that the need for action was great, and time was short. We cannot – by availing ourselves of the calm perspective of hindsight – now say that, at that time, these actions were unjustified.

The dissenting justices were harsh: This is a case "of convicting a citizen as punishment for not submitting to imprisonment in a concentration camp . . . solely because of his ancestry, without evidence or inquiry concerning his loyalty and good disposition towards the United States."

It was not until decades later that the U.S. began to look at itself in the mirror. In 1976, President Gerald Ford officially rescinded Roosevelt's Executive Order, calling the internment a "national mistake." In 1988, President Ronald Reagan signed the Civil Liberties Act, providing $20,000 in reparations to each surviving detainee. More importantly, the Act said what everyone knew to be true: the policy of internment was based on "race prejudice, war hysteria and a failure of political leadership" and not any genuine threat. Finally, the Act asked the Attorney General to review any criminal convictions of those who refused to relocate to the internment camps and recommend pardons to the President.

The 1988 Act, however, was not necessary to vacate Fred Korematsu's conviction. In 1980, President Jimmy Carter created the Commission on Wartime Relocation and Internment of Civilians. Convened to review the facts and circumstances of Executive Order 9066 and the proclamations and orders which sprung from it, the Commission was comprised of former members of Congress, the Supreme Court and the Cabinet, among others. Its findings were unanimous – at the time Roosevelt's executive order was issued, there was "substantial credible evidence" contradicting the justification for military exclusion and internment of Japanese Americans. Rather, "broad historical causes which shaped these decisions were race prejudice, war hysteria and a failure of political leadership." The Commission concluded that the incarceration which took place in response to Executive Order 9066 was a "grave injustice."

At about the same time, University of California San Diego professor Peter Irons and researcher Aiko Herzig-Yoshinaga came upon

Justice Department documents while researching government archives. Among the documents were memos written in 1943 and 1944 by Edward Ennis, the U.S. Justice Department attorney responsible for supervising the drafting of the government's brief. He was unable to defend the military's claim that incarceration of Japanese Americans was justified – indeed, a number of government intelligence agencies categorically denied that Japanese Americans had committed any wrong doing. These reports – over the objection of Ennis, a memo later found tells us – were never presented to the U.S. Supreme Court, having been intentionally suppressed.

Thus, in 1984, Korematsu sought to have his conviction vacated based on an arcane legal theory (writ of *coram nobis*, or writ of error) which allows the court to act if there was an unknown, fundamental error which did not appear in the original proceedings – here, government misconduct. Based on the Commission Report, and the clear evidence that the government "knowingly withheld" documents and information concerning its consideration of whether the camps were a "military necessity" at the time of the proclamations and orders, the California district court vacated Korematsu's conviction.

The California judge well-described the Supreme Court's decision, which, the California decision notwithstanding:

> . . .stands as law of the case and for whatever precedential value it may
> still have. Justices of the Supreme Court and legal scholars have com-
> mented that the decision is an anachronism in upholding overt racial
> discrimination as 'compellingly justified'. . . Korematsu remains on the
> pages of our legal and political history. As a legal precedent it is now
> recognized as having very limited application. As historical precedent
> it stands as a constant caution that in times of war or declared military
> necessity our institutions must be vigilant in protecting constitutional
> guarantees. It stands as a caution that in times of distress the shield of
> military necessity and national security must not be used to protect

governmental actions from close scrutiny and accountability. It stands as a caution that in times of international hostility and antagonisms our institutions, legislative, executive and judicial, must be prepared to exercise their authority to protect all citizens from the petty fears and prejudices that are so easily aroused.

In 1998, Fred Toyosaburo Korematsu, who had remained an activist throughout his life, was awarded the Presidential Medal of Freedom, the nation's highest civilian honor, from President Bill Clinton. The proclamation describes, "[a]n American who only wanted to be treated like any other American, Fred T. Korematsu challenged our nation's conscience, reminding us that we must uphold the rights of our own citizens even as we fight tyranny in other lands."

Seventy-three years after the U.S. Supreme Court upheld Korematsu's conviction, the Court decided *Trump v. Hawaii*, where the Court found 5-4 that President Donald Trump's executive order restricting travel into the country could proceed. The dissenting justices invoked *Korematsu*. Chief Justice John Roberts, Jr., who wrote the five-person majority decision, disagreed that it was relevant, but attacked the case head on:

> The forcible relocation of U. S. citizens to concentration camps, solely and explicitly on the basis of race, is objectively unlawful and outside the scope of Presidential authority. *** The dissent's reference to Korematsu . . . affords this Court the opportunity to make express what is already obvious: Korematsu was gravely wrong the day it was decided, has been overruled in the court of history, and—to be clear—"has no place in law under the Constitution." [quoting from the *Korematsu* dissent].

A footnote: Japanese nationals (known as Issei – first generation) were not eligible to become naturalized citizens until 1952, well after the

War. Korematsu's mother, Kotsui, did not live to see that day – she died in 1951. His father, Kakusaburo, became a naturalized citizen on February 7, 1954, at the age of 77, pledging allegiance to the government that had detained him a decade earlier.

DISCUSSION

One might try to understand, at least by 1942 standards, why the U.S. military might have been concerned about someone who came to the United States from Japan at the time of the Pearl Harbor attack. But we cannot escape looking at this through today's prism when the U.S. president says of four U.S. congresswomen – three born here and one a naturalized citizen who has lived here since she was a child – "Why don't they go back and help fix the totally broken and crime infested places from which they came. Then come back and show us how it is done."

Fred Korematsu's parents lived here; they contributed to the U.S. in every way a citizen would. Yet, they were not even permitted to take the oath of citizenship until 1952 (after Fred's mother had died). For Fred (and three of our congresswomen), there was no oath to take. They were born here. He was accorded the "freedom" from taking an oath of allegiance.

But what did that really mean? Ostensibly, he had the privilege to live anywhere in the U.S. and do anything any other citizen could do. Except, when Fred Korematsu in fact tried to join the armed forces to protect his country, he was turned away because of his ancestry. And when he sought to live where he had always lived, the military deemed it a zone in which no Japanese-Americans could live.

Why did the government conclude that Fred Korematsu posed a risk? It didn't. It never looked at Korematsu or any other individual.

Rather, it concluded that all persons of Japanese ancestry within its new military zones were suspect and thus, without any kind of individualized review, removed them all to internment camps.

But suppose Korematsu, or any individual born within the United States, was required at age 18 to take the same oath of allegiance as do naturalized citizens. It seems that, based on the now-disdained moment in our history described above, the oath obligation wouldn't have mattered anyway. Meaning, if someone simply "looked" like Fred Korematsu, taking an oath wouldn't have given his sworn promise any gravitas whatsoever – presumably, even if his ancestors had been here for five generations. Indeed, had Korematsu publicly (and sincerely) denounced the Emperor of Japan and his personal allegiance to him and the Empire, the United States military would nonetheless have rejected his ability to reside on the West Coast, ostensibly fearing that he would possibly still be secretly aligned with the enemy.

So here is a question. If a new citizen must take an oath of allegiance to their new country, doesn't that country owe them something in return? In other words, doesn't the country owe to its new citizens the same commitment it has to its natural-born citizens?

The value of an oath – or even a birthright – relies not only on the credibility of the individual who has given it, but also on the credibility of the one who has administered the oath.

Inasmuch as this is a book about oaths and Fred Korematsu was never required to take one, how does the obligation of an oath actually apply here? If one thinks about it, even though the Supreme Court never discussed it in these terms, wasn't there, or shouldn't there have been, an "implied oath" on the part of the United States benefitting Korematsu? Indeed, from the moment of his birth, he was a citizen of the United States – as much a citizen as anyone else who held that status beginning with those who arrived at Plymouth Rock. Accordingly, didn't the United States have *an obligation flowing toward him* just the same as if he were a child of George Washington or perhaps another Founder of this nation? Just imagine a descendent of Lafayette being hauled off to an American detention camp based on a state of war existing between the United States and France. What the government did to Korematsu, allowing him to be a citizen but only *where and how* it was acceptable to the government, rendered him a *second-class* citizen. Meaning, for the government, one was only a full citizen as long as his ancestors weren't born in Japan (or in whatever country appeared to pose a security risk to the United States).

And that is the nub of such an implied oath – that there is a duty that should flow from our nation to the citizen. It is a duty imposed on the nation for every individual who is a citizen of the United States.

CHAPTER EIGHT
The Clergy

Father Joseph Towle

All religious leaders vow to abide by the tenets of their religion. It is their sacred oath. Catholic priests take vows of poverty, celibacy, and obedience, i.e., they work for the betterment of the community and not themselves, all in dedication to the church. "I shall follow and foster the common discipline of the entire Church and I shall maintain the observance of all ecclesiastical laws, especially those contained in the Code of Canon Law."

When it comes to confidentiality of confession, it is different indeed as it's violation may severely impact another person, and the priest's decision to violate the oath may severely impact society in general. The Code of Canon Law well describes the obligations:

> The sacramental seal is inviolable; therefore it is absolutely forbidden
> for a confessor to betray in any way a penitent in words or in any
> manner and for any reason.

***

A confessor is prohibited completely from using knowledge acquired from confession to the detriment of the penitent even when any danger of revelation is excluded.

A person who has been placed in authority cannot use in any manner for external governance the knowledge about sins which he has received in confession at any time.

Code of Canon Law §§ 983, 984.

So essential is the seal of confession, that priests cannot reveal what they have learned to anyone, even if there is a threat of death to themselves or others. Indeed, the purpose of the confessional is to "protect the penitent from betrayal by the revelation of his confessional matter. . ."

A priest who breaks his vow of confidentiality would be excommunicated absent absolution granted by the Holy See. As St. Thomas Aquinas explained, a priest hears confession "not as a man, but as God knows it." Thus, it is the priest who, as a conduit, can grant absolution to a penitent who has sincerely, and with contrition, confessed his sins. And this is precisely why a Catholic would confess to a priest. It is the priest who embodies the fundamental Catholic belief that all sins can be forgiven and that there is nothing so terrible that it can't be confessed to a priest in the sanctity of the confessional, where what is said will never be revealed.

The requirement that the clergy maintain the confidences of their parishioners was not always protected by secular law. New York was the first state in America to implement a statute protecting priest-penitent communications in 1813. A priest at St. Peter's Catholic Church returned some stolen goods to their rightful owner, but refused to divulge who gave them to him, citing the seal of the confessional. The court refused to require the priest to testify. Not because the court wanted to protect congregants who confessed to their priests; rather, the court was concerned about protecting the priest from being forced to serve two masters – from having to choose between secular and religious law:

> We are of opinion that such a witness ought not to be compelled to answer. The benevolent and just principles of the common law, guard with the most scrupulous circumspection, against temptations to perjury, and against a violation of moral feeling; and what greater inducement can there be for the perpetration of this offence, than placing a man between Scylla and Charybdis, and in such an awful dilemma that he must either violate his oath, or proclaim his infamy in the face of day, and in the presence of a scoffing multitude?

This "priest-penitent" privilege was codified in New York 15 years later, and other states followed; it was eventually made applicable to all clergy.

THE STORY

The Code of Canon Law is harsh: "It is absolutely forbidden for a confessor to betray in any way a penitent in words or in any manner and for any reason." Does this mean that innocent men must sit in jail or even face death when the penitent who actually committed the crime feels profound guilt, but decides to follow the advice of his lawyer and remain silent no matter his priest's guidance? Such is the distinction between lawyers and priests – the lawyer sees the picture solely through the needs and lens of the client; the priest's conduct is compelled by a greater (shall we call it) constituency.

Father Joseph Towle was a Roman Catholic priest who led his flock in the Hunts Point section of Bronx, New York. In 1987, there was a brutal murder – Jose Antonio Rivera, Jennifer Rodriguez and her 11-year-old son were walking when they saw a group of teenagers, at least one of whom was holding a baseball bat or a stick. Rivera ran, the teenagers caught up to him, beat him with the bat and repeatedly stabbed him. A few days later, Jose Morales, age 18, was placed in a lineup and Rodriguez identified him as one of the teenagers. Morales and one other, Ruben Montalvo, were later convicted of murdering Rivera.

After they were convicted, but before they were sentenced, Jesus Fornes went to Father Towle. They were not in the formalized setting of the confessional, but Fornes told Father Towle that Montalvo and Morales were simply not present when Rivera was killed, and he definitely knew this because it was he and two others who actually committed the murder. Fornes was distressed; he asked Father Towle what he should do. Father Towle told him that if he "had the courage and heart to do it, that he should go to court and [] acknowledge that he was responsible, and the others were not." Towle granted Fornes absolution, a "pardon in the name of God for the things that he had done wrong."

Fornes, troubled by his own silence even though he was a murderer, and abiding Father Towle's advice, went to Montalvo's mother and told her what really happened. She called her son's lawyer, and Morales's mother. Fornes told his story to Montalvo's lawyer immediately before Montalvo and Morales were about to be sentenced. He said: "I did the crime; I will do the time. They did nothing. They weren't even there." The lawyer arranged to have the sentencing hearing adjourned, apparently to have time to speak more fully with Fornes, believing that Fornes would testify and tell the truth – that his client was innocent.

Fornes got nervous; he was obviously scared. So rather than meet with Montalvo's lawyer, as had been arranged, Father Towle went with Fornes to a local Legal Aid office, where Fornes met with attorney Stanley Cohen alone. Years later, Cohen recalled Fornes's state of mind:

"I can't sleep, can't eat, no one has forced me or paid me or told me to do this, just something wrong has happened."

Cohen is a lawyer. His job – his institutional oath – was to his client, *and only his client*. He told Fornes, in effect, "you are 18, if you tell this you will throw your life away, and it may not do your friends any good. You should do nothing – take the Fifth Amendment." And he well-expressed that difference between lawyers and the clergy:

> If you feel guilt, you have the priest here. You can feel guilt with the priest.

Cohen spoke to the prosecutor, and to defense counsel. He became convinced that if Fornes testified truthfully, he would accomplish nothing for his friends, and would himself end up in jail along with them for life. On Cohen's advice, Fornes declined to answer any questions when called to the stand at Montalvo and Morales's sentencing.

Father Towle corresponded with Morales while he was in prison. There is nothing to indicate that Father Towle revealed what Fornes had told him. But Father Towle did consider whether there was some way, "within the framework of Catholic practice" to tell what Fornes confessed. Fornes died in 1997, ten years after he committed that brutal murder, for reasons unrelated to Morales or Montalvo. Father Towle, Montalvo and Morales having already served ten years in jail, wanted to tell what he had learned from Fornes a decade earlier. Searching his religious and moral convictions, and his memory, the Father concluded that his conversation with Fornes was not a "formal confession," so that the disclosure of Fornes's statements would not violate his sacramental oath. In 2000, Towle finally told Morales's lawyer what Fornes had told him all those years earlier.

According to the writings of St. Thomas Aquinas, a Sacramental Confession has three parts – contrition (the penitent's willingness to atone); confession (that he submit to the judgment of the priest standing in God's place); and satisfaction (that he atone according to the decision of God's minister). The priest then grants absolution. While reasonable people may debate whether Fornes's statements constituted a Sacramental Confession as that term is understood in Catholicism, Father Towle consulted the legal department of the Archdiocese of New York, which agreed with Father Towle, and countenanced his action in deciding to disclose Fornes's statements.

Father Towle, now deceased, described his own struggle, and why it took him so long to come forward:

> There is nothing I am more careful about in my whole life than the confessional secret and therefore I reflected on the basis, if there were any basis on which I could reveal the fact that . . . Jesus Fornes had spoken to me and eventually I made the judgment, yes, that I could, because I believed it was not a formal confession . . .
>
> ***
>
> Now, in the course of time I have had to reflect a great deal . . . but at that time I think all would [have] understood that if someone were to come to a Catholic priest and to confess to a murder in a confessional situation which is between that person and God, using myself in this case as a medium, that there is nothing absolutely that I could ever say.

In 2001, the state courts having declined to right the wrong that resulted at the trial of Montalvo and Morales, the case came before (then) United States District Judge Denny Chin who, among many other procedural issues, had to overcome a secular/non-secular hurdle. Under New York law, a member of the clergy may not disclose a "confession or confidence made to him in his professional character as spiritual advisor." Thus, could the judge allow testimony if it was barred by statute? Ultimately, Judge Chin concluded that he was in no position to second guess Father Towle, who said the discussion with Fornes was not a "formal confession," or the Archdiocese, which found that Father Towle acted properly in disclosing the conversation. Given that, and that Fornes told at least parts of his story to Montalvo's mother and others, the court concluded that Fornes acted in a manner inconsistent with any desire to maintain a priest-penitent privilege, and in effect waived that privilege. Montalvo and Morales were finally released, 13 years after their conviction, for a crime they didn't commit; a crime that they literally had nothing to do with.

DISCUSSION

Let's look at the Fornes case through a broader scope. If you choose to confide something horrible that you have done (or even have been the victim of) in your lifetime to a confidante, e.g., a friend, a mentor, or even a spouse, for whatever reason you choose to reveal it or however tied you are to the confidante, you knowingly risk a future collapse in your relationship with that person (indeed, perhaps even because of the disclosure). Or perhaps you misperceived from the outset the very integrity of the individual confided in as worthy of your confidence. Or maybe you didn't fully appreciate that the recipient of the confidence you shared wouldn't recognize the weightiness *to you* of maintaining the secrecy of what you chose to disclose. Or maybe they believe that your desire for confidentiality was simply wrongheaded and that you – indeed, *you* – actually *need* for them to disclose it.

The personal betrayal that you experienced when you learned that the confidence was broken and revealed without your "authorization," however, has no legal force or efficacy. Put simply, when you made the private revelation truly believing that not "in a million years" would it be disclosed by your supposed confidante, you knew, or you should have known, that nothing other than the confidante's good faith or allegiance to you could be relied on to commit him to silence about it *in the future* – indeed forever. Even if the confidante went so far as to "promise" you that nothing you told them would be in turn revealed, you would simply be out of luck, even if the promise figuratively made on a stack of bibles was false *ab initio*. Some miscarriages in life are not remediable by the law – even if the promisor's conduct in "promising" confidentiality is spurious. Your remedy *on this earth*, as it were, lies perhaps only in personal animus, vendetta or vengeance. For those breaches of your privacy, there is no true curative.

Let's put aside the law and speak only of the priest's duty of maintaining a penitent's confidentiality. And let's change the facts involving Fornes to a circumstance where there was indeed a formal confession by him to Father Towle – within the actual physical confines of the confessional booth. According to Father Towle's testimony – presumably based on canonical doctrine and advice – he would have been absolutely enjoined from revealing what Fornes had confided in him. Even if Fornes was truly remorseful, but yet unwilling to expose himself to life in prison, Father Towle would have been precluded from doing anything to right the colossal wrong of the admittedly unjust convictions of Morales and Montalvo.

Accepting for these purposes that a priest is indeed God's representative on earth (for Catholics) and without intending to challenge the church doctrine that created that sanctity of the confessional, one must wonder about the value in terms of the sanctity of human life and freedom that would allow an extreme injustice to prevail in the name of confidentiality for the penitent? Yes, any society, religious or secular, wants to encourage a despairing person – such as one who needs or even simply wants to confess it – to reveal his or her act of immorality or "sin." Still, should society also want the priest to be oath-bound to maintain that confidence, even if an injustice will be perpetrated against others by virtue of that confidentiality?

Not only that, but unlike the willingness of lawyers (such as Staples Hughes (see "The Lawyer")) to depart from their confidentiality obligation after the death of the confessing client, it seems clear – Father Towle, in particular, testified so – that if he had received the Fornes confession in the confessional, a priest would have been obligated to strictly and unwaveringly adhere to the duty of confidentiality even after Fornes died. While not intending to challenge in any way the church's teaching on the subject, how does this make sense in terms of the aim of a religion that surely wants to do good?

Of course, if one has been unfaithful to his wife or privately cursed God and feels genuine remorse over his sin, there is great benefit – and seemingly no corresponding detriment – for the confessing individual to make the disclosure to a confidante, in this case a priest, who promises confidentiality. But in the Fornes/Towle case, the penitent's disclosure to the priest would enable the priest to actually cure an injustice. Who is served by placing the seal on that? What religious value desirable to the church is furthered by the requirement of non-disclosure, when any rational person would see the curing of an injustice to be the ultimate value? Does it suggest that an oath of confidentiality taken by a priest simply cannot be understood in current means of thinking? Again, we speak not of a circumstance where there is great value in encouraging a believer to "confess" or for other believers to know in their hearts that the priest is good to his word – that is, in circumstances where no one can be helped by the disclosure. Fornes is indeed such a case where an injustice could have been avoided.

One can understand why the law would want to enforce the priestly confession given "freedom of religion" principles, when taping shut a priest's mouth won't cause *future* harm to individuals. So, let's go to a variation on the theme. What about when the priest receives information from a penitent that suggests that the penitent will sin again, the sin being criminal in nature?

Let's take Fornes's case uphill where the oxygen is thinner. Suppose a wayward (hypothetical) priest who has abused several altar boys goes to confession – formal confession. With great remorsefulness, he speaks across the latticed opening in the confessional booth and tells his sins. He promises to never do it again. While the confessor priest fully accepts the genuineness of the penitent's remorse, as might anyone listening to this particular penitent's description of what he had done and his existential sadness over it, given some of the thoughts he expresses, *anyone* would also recognize that this priest's days of such sexual abuse are hardly over. He will surely "sin" again in precisely the same way, but now with new victims!

Father Towle said that the venue, if it is that, of the confessional booth – rather than in Fornes's case of a "Come to Jesus" meeting – would have sealed his lips. Indeed, the sacredness of his oath of confidentiality would have been inviolable. And American law would protect that inviolability. However, how are we to view an oath, however well-intentioned, that denies the priest the ability to protect boys who stand to be sexually abused in the future by disclosing to the authorities what the priest has done, and what he reasonably believes the priest will do if not removed from his post? Confessing here no scholarship on the subject, it seems that even if the confessor wanted to bring the issue to his fellow priests to conduct an "intervention" of sorts for the offender in order to right his ship, such an action, too, would be impermissible. Not to mention the extreme circumstance where the "victim" of the offending priest comes to confession and feeling personal guilt as having been an enabler – not an unusual psychological result – insists that the confessor priest maintain his silence.

Indeed, Australia is trying to address the priest abuse crisis by a series of reforms, including legally requiring priests to report abuse to police – even when it is revealed during confession. As of this writing, the leaders of the Catholic church in Australia agree with several non-secular recommendations, but not that priests may report what is told to them in confession: the seal of confession is "a non-negotiable element of [Catholic] religious life and embodies an understanding of the believer and God."

Interestingly, the Jewish religion doesn't see it the same way. No rabbi takes an oath, as does a priest, when he is ordained. Of course, it is understood that he or she will exercise extreme discretion in dealing with the private communications of their congregants, and congregants expect confidentiality when disclosing their "issues" to the rabbi. But rabbis don't receive confession in the same way as do priests. Indeed, some interpretations of the Talmud *require* that rabbis disclose confidences. And because there is no hierarchy within the Jewish religion as to how rabbis should act in dealing with the secular world, how they act is individualized. Some will treat the congregant's confession, as it were, in the same way as might a priest who hears confession in the confessional booth. Some will weigh the severity of the offense in deciding whether to disclose to the authorities, or to the victim of the confessant's wrongdoing. Some will examine the moral imperative involved and decide simply based on their assessment of "what's right." Is it better to have a strict oath as do Catholic priests, or better for the clergy to maintain the discretion (or is malleability?) to decide for oneself?

What happens, under state law, when a rabbi – who has never taken such an oath – indeed reveals information his congregant believed she was disclosing confidentially? Chani Lightman was an observant Jew who was seeking a divorce and custody of her children. She spoke with two rabbis who were her spiritual leaders. She told them she had stopped engaging in certain religious practices involving menstrual purity and – even though still married – she was seeing another man in a social setting. The rabbis not only disclosed the secrets she told them, they submitted signed statements for her husband to use in their custody battle. Indeed, one of the rabbis opined that not only did she no longer wish to strictly adhere to Jewish law, she did not want her children to do so either.

Lightman sued the rabbis for breaching their duty to her and for inflicting emotional distress upon her – they disclosed confidences that she intended be secret. From a legal perspective, she argued, a civil statute says that a member of the clergy shall not be allowed to disclose a "confession or confidence made to him in his professional character . . ." and the rabbis violated that statute. But New York's highest court dismissed the lawsuit. The statute, it held, determines whether evidence is admissible in court – not whether the rabbis can be sued for breaching a duty if they reveal what was said to them, however confidential their congregant believed the conversation to be.

So, where does this end up? No one should challenge the church's decision that historically gave priests the ability to accord absolution to its sinners, and to do so within the framework of the sacrament of confession. There is great psychological – maybe religious – benefit in a penitent coming to terms with his sinfulness and promising to never repeat his transgression; and in some circumstances it is also healthy for society, particularly if the confessed sin constitutes a crime.

The Fornes case was decided based on the technicality that Fornes's "conversation" with Father Towles didn't qualify as a confession, thus not warranting the "seal." But imagine what that oath might have meant to the two actual innocents if a confession (within the confessional) had been made by Fornes, and Fornes had not disclosed his guilt to the families of Morales and Montalvo suggesting that he was willing to come forward. Imagine further, that the innocents were facing – or had already faced – the death penalty. How troubling would full compliance with that sacrament have been?

Especially for non-Catholics who don't have it, the concept of a person having a human intermediary who possesses the capacity to extend absolution of behalf of God is appealing indeed. For he is an "emissary" who, in the Catholic tradition, essentially speaks on God's behalf and awards the penitent greater confidence that the request for absolution is actually accepted. And likewise, it is essential that the penitent who may be disclosing something horrendous "know" that his disclosure will remain forever within the priest's mind – no memorandum on file, no cc to another parish priest seeking advice whether absolution is warranted.

The scenario where *a priest* confesses within the confessional words that suggest that the confessing priest may actually "sin" again, may be an outlier indeed. It is, however, the outlier that validates the sanctity of the oath of silence. As the church apparently sees it, despite the explosive clergy scandals of this century, creating exceptions to allow disclosure where the confession essentially admits the likelihood of future criminality by the confessing priest, risks a troubling slippery slope. It is this slippery slope argument that has apparently persuaded the church that the sanctity of the sacramental oath would be devastated in the event of departure from the rigid teaching of the Code of Canon Law.

We try to understand and articulate here, however imperfectly, the church's doctrine; not to challenge it.

CHAPTER NINE
The Journalist

Judith Miller

THE OATH

Given the brutal murders of journalists Daniel Pearl – an American – of *The Wall Street Journal* and, more recently, Jamal Khashoggi – a Saudi, but an American resident – of *The Washington Post*, precisely for their journalistic efforts, there is great alarm over the potential danger to American journalists who carry out their reportorial function, particularly when it relates to investigations involving international intrigue in the non-democratic world.

And while the Pearl and Khashoggi murders did not, as far as we can tell, directly involve it, for an investigative journalist there is no more sacred oath than to protect their confidential source. As Judith Miller, the subject of our story, once testified: "Confidential sources are the life's blood of journalism."

The right to a free press is embedded in the First Amendment to the Constitution – "Congress shall make no law . . . abridging the freedom of speech, or of the press . . ."

But the Constitution did not answer the question of whether a journalist may be required to identify his source, or provide information given to him confidentially. There have been attempts to get journalists to name names, as it were, since Colonial times. In the late 1800's John

Morris, a reporter for *The Baltimore Sun*, refused to identify his source in a story about bribery of public officials to a grand jury. Morris spent two days in jail, and in response, the Maryland legislature passed a law barring the issuance of subpoenas to reporters – meaning, reporters would not be forced to disclose their confidential sources.

Three decades later, a *New York Tribune* reporter who wrote about customs smugglers argued that there was – or should be – a "reporter's privilege." He lost in the courts, but not in popular opinion so that, eventually, a number of state legislatures passed laws protecting reporters, similar to Maryland's.

Journalists might promise sources confidentiality for myriad reasons but, at bottom, it is to make sure they get their story. But what is it that binds a journalist to that pledge? Some news organizations leave it up to the individual reporter; some have a policy strictly prohibiting reporters from disclosing information once confidentiality was promised.

The issue of reporters' promises of confidentiality remained fairly dormant until the 1970s, when federal prosecutors began issuing subpoenas to journalists, demanding information about criminal activity they reported, and about dissident groups and their whereabouts. The reason is that journalists often gain access to locations and information that law enforcement does not have – and they are given that access because the groups trust that the reporter's vow of confidentiality has meaning.

Three cases made their way to the U.S. Supreme Court in 1972 – in one, a reporter wrote a story about hashish production in Kentucky; in the other two, reporters had much-desired information about the Black Panther movement. The Court decided *Branzburg v. Hayes,* in a 5-4 decision that is still being debated today. It found that – constitutionally – a compelling and paramount state interest is served when reporters are required to disclose confidential information to grand juries.

The federal courts have thus rejected an argument that journalists enjoy First Amendment protections, i.e., that they are automatically constitutionally protected from having to testify regarding confidential information. The question of whether, if the journalist promises confidentiality, there is some federal, common law privilege remains in play. Indeed, in the *Miller* case, the judges of the federal appellate court, the D.C. Circuit, couldn't agree on whether a common law privilege even exists, although all concluded that, even if it did, there was no basis to apply it there. As one judge noted, the special counsel had demonstrated, among other things, the need for the information that Miller possessed, and that it could not be obtained elsewhere.

The states, however, fall on the side of journalists – all but Wyoming have statutory or common law versions of the "Shield Law." Premised on the importance of providing a generous climate for the free exchange of ideas, the Shield Laws protect reporters from having to testify if they promised their source confidentiality. Each state is different – in some, like New York, there is an "absolute" privilege if the reporter promised confidentiality; once a promise of confidentiality is made, the reporter cannot be required to testify. Period.

THE STORY

Which brings us to investigative reporter Judith Miller, who put her own safety at risk, and her life on hold, to protect her source.

Miller's story centers on perhaps the most well-known, politically charged, modern-day challenge to a reporter's right to keep her source confidential. It is a twisting story, to be sure; one in which we may never know all of the facts. Let's set the stage. It is early 2002. The U.S. had been attacked, viciously and on our own soil, on September 11, 2001. "9/11" was still raw, and the government was struggling with how to address the aftermath of the attacks – not from a domestic front; but rather how to ensure that those responsible for the attack paid a price.

In February 2002, at the request of the CIA, former ambassador Joseph Wilson traveled to Niger to investigate claims that Iraq had purchased yellowcake uranium – necessary for the production of "weapons of mass destruction" (WMDs). He returned and reported (as we now know) that there was indeed no evidence that Niger was producing uranium for sale to Iraq. Yet, in March 2003, the U.S. nonetheless invaded Iraq on the stated premise that it was in fact manufacturing and in possession of WMDs. Indeed, President George W. Bush's January 2003 State of the Union included these now-famous words: "The British government has learned Saddam Hussein has recently sought significant quantities of uranium from Africa," a statement that we since learned was, at best, an embellishment.

On July 6, 2003, Wilson wrote an op-ed for *The New York Times*, entitled "What I Didn't Find in Africa." If the title weren't enough, the piece began with the heated question: "Did the Bush Administration manipulate intelligence about Saddam Hussein's weapons programs to justify an invasion of Iraq?" Wilson concluded that, based on his personal experience – which he detailed – the U.S. government's intelligence concerning Iraq was "twisted to exaggerate" the threat.

To remember where the country was at the time, the U.S. populace was sharply divided over the war in Iraq. Some (perhaps all) would say that Wilson's piece only added fuel to the fire. And then on July 14, conservative political commentator and columnist Robert Novak revealed in his *Chicago Sun Times* and *Wall Street Journal* syndicated columns that Wilson's wife, Valerie Plame, "is a [CIA] operative on weapons of mass destruction." Matthew Cooper, of *Time*, similarly identified Plame. There were also reports (speculation, perhaps), that Plame was working on WMDs and was responsible for sending Wilson to Niger in the first place.

Was the Bush administration, or at least some of its supporters, getting back at Wilson, somehow? Did it "out" Wilson's wife and create a national security nightmare so that she and other CIA operatives were compromised and in potential physical danger? Such was the conjecture and the ever-present news cycle talked about it for weeks, if not months.

Now, it is a crime under certain circumstances to reveal the identity of a CIA operative. So on December 30, 2003, the Attorney General appointed Patrick Fitzgerald as special counsel and a grand jury was convened to investigate exactly who in government disclosed Plame's identity.

Journalists – at least good journalists – take their pledge of confidentiality extremely seriously. The White House understood this but was insistent that the source of the leak be found – President Bush would not permit anyone to hide behind a journalist's promise. He announced that, if there was a leak from the White House, he wanted to know! Indeed, that leaker would "no longer work in my administration." Thus, anyone and everyone who worked in the White House was required to waive confidentiality if they had spoken to a reporter identifying Plame. No exceptions. The president could not compel a journalist to disclose her source, but he could compel each of his subordinates to reveal if he or she was the source – at penalty of firing if they declined, and maybe criminal referral.

How exactly does that bring us to Judith Miller and *The New York Times*, the publication she worked for at the time? Miller in fact never wrote a story about Plame; but she did report on the "U.S. Hunt for Hussein's Chemical and Germ Weapons." And she had spoken to officials about Wilson – his disclosures about Niger and that he was married to Plame. But how did Fitzgerald know this? In truth, Miller was already on his radar in a totally unrelated matter. He, as U.S. Attorney for Northern Illinois, had been aggressively investigating two Islamic charities, which the government suspected had terrorist ties. Fitzgerald had (successfully, albeit years later in 2006) demanded Miller's home, office and cell phone records in connection with that investigation. Now, in his role as special counsel in the Plame Affair, as it is known, he was also looking to Miller.

Fitzgerald spoke with and subpoenaed several reporters to testify before his grand jury. Matthew Cooper, a *Time* journalist, initially refused to testify. He was held in contempt by a federal court on the application of Fitzgerald, yet he avoided jail because he – relying on the Bush White House-ordered blanket waiver – identified his source as senior presidential advisor Karl Rove and delivered his notes to Fitzgerald. Novak, for his part, confirmed that Rove was one of his sources. Another – Deputy Secretary of State Richard Armitage, who was a fierce anti-war advocate – actually admitted that he was Novak's primary source.

One might have thought that Cooper's disclosure, with Novak's confirmation and Armitage's admission, would be enough. But no. Fitzgerald was going to proceed, and Miller was one of the journalists subpoenaed to testify before a grand jury.

But Miller and her lawyer – the estimable Floyd Abrams, the leading First Amendment lawyer in America, who also represented *The New York Times* – concluded that her source's signature on the Bush-ordered, generic, blanket waiver was not a voluntary statement by him authorizing her to testify. If, in her mind, not a truly voluntary waiver, Miller simply would not identify him – she had promised him confidentiality. And, as she told Judge Thomas Hogan of the U.S. District Court for the District of Columbia at the time when he held her in contempt:

> If journalists cannot be trusted to keep confidences, then journalists
> cannot function and there cannot be a free press.

Miller, having lost her appeal to the appeals court – in furtherance of her fervent belief in the promises journalists make to their sources – spent 85 days in the Alexandria Virginia City Jail beginning in July 2005, until she received what she believed was in fact an un-coerced and voluntary waiver from her source – I. Lewis "Scooter" Libby, then Chief of Staff to Vice President Dick Cheney. Once she had that waiver (and a letter from Libby essentially authorizing her to testify), and after full compliance with her journalist's oath, she was released from prison and testified before the grand jury, and years later at the *Libby* obstruction/perjury trial.

But there is more to the story. As we now know, Plame, despite the legitimate fear that her status as a CIA operative would endanger her, turned out not to be in danger as a result of her identity being leaked. Also, Fitzgerald knew, from as early as 2003, that it was Armitage who gave Novak her name. But yet Fitzgerald seemingly needed his pound of flesh, and for reasons, totally unclear even today, he did not go after Rove or Armitage. No. After Miller testified that Libby told her about Plame's identity, Fitzgerald went after Libby.

Now Libby was never charged with having outed Plame; no one was. Rather, he was indicted and convicted of obstruction of justice and perjury. You see, Libby had told federal investigators and testified before the grand jury that he (Libby) had been told by a journalist (not Miller) that all reporters knew Plame was a CIA operative. When called to testify at Libby's trial, however, that journalist, NBC Bureau Chief Tim Russert, was clear that Plame's name never came up in any conversation he had with Libby.

Libby's trial was held in 2007 – some four years after Miller's discussions with him. Miller was one of ten journalists who testified, and since she was the only one to state that Libby discussed Plame, her testimony was essential. She was, in fact, Fitzgerald's star witness. This, even though Miller also testified that, while her notes reflected it, she did not actually recall Libby giving her Plame's name, or that Plame's job was secret, or that she helped send Wilson to Niger.

Libby was convicted and sentenced to 30 months. He served none of them, although he did pay a $250,000 fine. President Bush commuted his sentence immediately after it was imposed and, years later, President Trump pardoned him.

But the story continues. In 2015, Miller revealed in her book, *The Story: A Reporter's Journey*, that she now believes she was manipulated by Fitzgerald, that he withheld information from her, and that her recollection of her notes' meaning and her conversations with Libby – those she testified to – were incorrect. Indeed, as she later made clear, Libby never gave her Plame's name.

At the end of this long and winding tale, we are left with Judith Miller – the only person in this mess of a story who actually went to jail. And in doing so, she stood up for the constitutional rights of journalists and all who speak confidentially to them.

DISCUSSION

There is always a doctrinal reason why a recipient of a disclosure intended to remain secret is required to abide by his pledge. Physicians and attorneys want to encourage their patients or clients to be as forthcoming as possible in order to better, and more meaningfully, counsel them about their health or legal jeopardy. Clergy – particularly Catholic priests – accept disclosure from their confessants in an effort to counsel penance, and perhaps even extend absolution. These are surely important societal values.

But journalists are different. Their oath of confidentiality is considerably different. The reporter – and her publication – make the decision of whether to agree to confidentiality on a case-by-case basis. If you are a source, you must specifically ask that your identity and your information, particularly if it is singular in nature, remain confidential, and the reporter must agree. Without that, there is no obligation. Yes, different from a doctor, a lawyer or the clergy – for them there is no requirement of a specific pledge.

In considering whether to agree to confidentiality, many report-ers – good reporters – will look at the information being offered, and perhaps the "leaker's" reasons for providing it. There are confidential "sources" who make disclosures to journalists to advance the true values of the body politic, or at least *their* body politic. Journalists often report breakdowns in government – today, particularly – based on con-fidential information. Even the courts acknowledge the importance of confidential sources:

> Without an unfettered press, citizens would be far less able to make
> informed political, social and economic choices. But the press' function
> as a vital source of information is weakened whenever the ability of
> journalists to gather news is impaired.

Such disclosures might report about problems at the White House, in the armed forces, in law enforcement, involving medical care and, indeed, regarding whether elections in the United States have been rigged by Russian spies. They also report gossip about celebrities – there is seemingly no true societal value at stake there. But often, per-haps too often, the sources who provide information to journalists do so for dubious reasons – jealously, political manipulation, or maybe even to stir up anarchy. The sources have truthful information which they intend to impart, but they are imparting it for arguably destruc-tive reasons, including personal advancement or self-aggrandizement. Yet once that pledge of confidentiality is made – of course the source has to know about the protocol to demand it – the journalist cannot disclose their source; that is, they must take the source's identity to the grave.

But why should the journalism profession accord confidentiality to sources when they end up – as they often know at the time – extending "pledges" to people who may be so ill-motivated? The *Plame/Wilson* case is the perfect case for the question. After all, one could argue that the disclosures to Novak, Cooper and Miller by White House employees were in retaliation for Wilson having told the truth – that there was no "yellow cake" needed to manufacture WMDs in Niger, contrary to the Bush pro-Iraq War party line which had justified U.S. entrance into that war. One could conclude that Ambassador Wilson had undermined the administration's story and embarrassed the administration in the process, so that there should be a price to pay for having done so – namely, his wife's safety. And maybe his own safety too. But even assuming the confidential sources weren't incentivized by high-minded inspiration, a journalist's oath is an oath, as Miller so exemplified by going to the wall and beyond for her source.

Interestingly, Miller essentially did what federal agents and police detectives do every day in promising confidentiality when receiving information from their high-level mafia "stoolpigeons" ("CIs" – confidential informants), who spill their guts about criminal enterprises conducted by their counterparts, often for the selfish purpose of eliminating the competition. The pledge of confidentiality to a source is as valid and warranting of confidentiality wherever the source might stand on the vast spectrum of how society values the person. Miller, like every journalist, would likely tell you it is not her desire or even duty to evaluate the motivation of the source, as long as the source is providing truthful, newsworthy information. He doesn't have to be "Deep Throat" or even in possession of the singular kind of information that Deep Throat possessed – information that brought down a president who had so violated a nation's trust.

Miller never published a story about what she had learned from Libby (or, at least, what she thought she learned from Libby) – yet Fitzgerald knew that Libby had spoken to her about it. So, while a grand jury is "entitled to everyman's evidence," why should a journalist have been put in the position of being ordered to make the disclosure in grand jury or trial testimony when she has given her word to the source?

If you were to ask Miller about that – about having had to spend 85 days in jail for her allegiance to her oath – she'd make clear that she's not bitter at all about it. She made a pledge and was obliged to comport with it, even though it seemed to most observers – but not Miller (or *The New York Times*) – that Libby had waived his confidentiality when President Bush issued an order directing blanket White House waivers. No, Miller is bitter only because she believes that Fitzgerald misled her so that she ultimately testified, in her view, incorrectly in a way that incriminated Libby.

Hardly anyone would disagree today that exposing the falsity in the Bush administration's supposed "proof" of WMDs in Iraq as a predicate for going to war would have warranted promises of confidentiality to knowledgeable sources in a position to disclose that falsity. The same as (today at least) virtually all would agree that a promise of confidentiality by *The New York Times* or *The Washington Post* to Daniel Ellsberg – who delivered to them, and the American people, the Pentagon Papers – was doing a great public service. When our government leads us into (or keeps us in) an unwise war based on false information, it is important that the electorate know it.

But why, one might ask – devil's advocate here – should journalists be free to promise and accomplish confidentiality, without any penalty to themselves, on behalf of those who are motivated by "foul" motive, and when the disclosures are not in the public interest? Could disclosure of the hardly scandalous fact that Valerie Plame was a CIA operative have possibly been in the public interest? Was the public interest served by potentiality jeopardizing the life of Wilson's wife as retaliation? Put simply, wouldn't the journalist's confidentiality obligation arising from affording anonymity to Libby (or Rove or Armitage) have raised the possibility of Plame becoming physically endangered, particularly if Miller had chosen to publish her "extra."

The difficulty with the pledge of confidentiality is that the law, in the view of some, simply shouldn't impose on journalists an added duty to psychologize the motivation of the source. There is a duty for mainstream publications to determine the merit of stories they publish and at the same time to determine if there are risks presented by their publication. A journalist embedded in war time would not report troop movements (remember Geraldo Rivera being "escorted" out of Iraq when he did just that); criminal liability potentially exists if they report classified information.

But short of that, there is no law which requires that journalists not make pledges of confidentiality, nor is there any law which says they may not abandon their pledges when the going gets rough and the courts determine that a greater good requires, under penalty of contempt (read, jail), that a journalist must testify. Yet journalists do make a pledge of confidentiality, and they do abide by it – regardless of their source's ideology, or reasons for coming forward. The "chill" that would be placed on journalists, and their sources, if they were to pick and choose when their pledge is binding, would be overwhelming.

Even though the laws do largely favor journalists, as we see in *Miller* it is not always so. There is thus a genuine problem with the pledge of confidentiality that a journalist makes when, and if, the courts get involved when a prosecutor insists that the information cannot be otherwise obtained and demands it by way of subpoena. Yes, if the court directs the testimony, the journalist has the ability to resist providing the identity of the declarant – but at a price: freedom. A journalist might see his oath in moral terms. Simply put, "I gave my word" – nothing more needs to be said about it. Or he might see it in martyr terms: "I'll become a big shot in the profession if I serve a brief stretch, letting future sources know I'll take a bullet for them." Or perhaps a journalist, willing to go to jail, likens himself to a hard-charging union leader who visualizes an occasional jail stretch as part of the cost of doing business.

No one wants to go to jail, but to a journalist the benefits of the experience might actually be worth the price. And whichever might be the motivating force in seeming to stand up for principle, the journalist is in fact complying with her oath – whether the public is in sync with her having made it or been willing to comply with it by paying the price in the face of a court order, or not.

Last point. The federal law, as applied in the *Miller* case, says in substance that the pledge of confidentiality that a reporter might make to a source can be overcome if the information imparted is critical to the investigation and cannot otherwise be obtained by the prosecutor – which apparently was the case in *Miller.* The law of many states, however, is that the pledge is absolute: if the information was imparted to the journalist under a confidentiality pledge, it is airtight.

So, for example, if the source – say, a confidant of Osama bin Laden – were, on September 6th, 2001, to have told a reporter *under a valid pledge of confidentiality* what would happen on September 11th, a *state* prosecutor could not compel disclosure of the source. This even if the reporter published a story on September 9th with great detail about what she was told (albeit without identifying her source) – and even despite the ticking time bomb information that she singularity has, needed to protect potential victims. Not so, however, under federal law – in these alarming circumstances a *federal* judge would throw the reporter in jail without a second thought.

CHAPTER TEN

THE JUROR

Julian Heicklen

THE OATH

Selected for jury duty, before the trial begins, the jurors will rise and raise their right hand. The judge, or clerk, will ask each juror to pledge – to take their oath – that they will act fairly and impartially, and that they will follow the law as it is explained by the judge. While different in each jurisdiction, jurors are asked:

> Do you and each of you solemnly swear [affirm] that you will well and truly try and a true deliverance make between the parties, and a true verdict render according to the law and evidence?

At the end of the trial, but before they begin deliberations, jurors may be told by the judge: "You are bound by the oath that you took at the beginning of the trial to follow the instructions that I give you, *even if you personally disagree with them.*"

So – a jury hears evidence, is advised of the law, and then renders a verdict, keeping the judge's instructions in mind. Clear as day, right? Not really. Sometimes jurors don't agree on credibility of witnesses, or on whether or how the testimony they have heard fits into the judge's instructions. Jurors may be unable to reach a verdict, adhering to instructions.

But sometimes jurors just conclude, for one reason or another, that the law is wrong. And they try to say so by their verdict. Courts are thus faced with the possibility of what is known as jury nullification. By consciously refusing to find a defendant guilty, the jury in effect "nullifies" the law that a defendant is accused of violating. In other words, a jury may, although clearly violating the court's instruction, return a verdict of "not guilty" despite clear and compelling evidence that the defendant committed the crime.

Sometimes there is jury nullification because the jury simply doesn't believe that the law should be the law, that the crime should be a crime. The jury may want to send a message about some social issue, or because the result required by law is contrary to the jury's sense of justice, morality or fairness. Would you convict someone for smoking marijuana on a street corner? What about gambling? Vagrancy? Would it make a difference if you knew the penalty to be imposed upon your finding of guilt would be five years of incarceration – even though jurors, according to case law, are never supposed to take into account the sentence?

Some people, typically libertarian-minded people – some distinguished judges and scholars – argue that jury nullification serves as a final check on the government's ability to enforce unjust laws; that it is a juror's constitutional right (duty, even) to decide which laws should be enforced, and against whom. Others, contrarily, argue that jurors are taking the law into their own hands – an act which would cause nothing less than chaos. For them, it is the legislature, not juries, that should repeal laws when they warrant repeal. Courts largely disfavor nullification, and at least one court has been clear that a jury simply has no right to find a guilty defendant not guilty, or a not guilty defendant guilty – "Such verdicts are lawless, a denial of due process and constitute an exercise of erroneously seized power."

Jury nullification, however, has been around for centuries. William Penn was arrested in 1670 England for unlawful assembly, i.e., for preaching Quakerism. There was really no dispute – all the prosecutor had to show was that Penn and others joined in a religious assembly not sanctioned by the Church of England. The jury, however, found Penn guilty of "speaking in Grace Church" and not unlawful assembly. Outraged by the verdict, the judge locked away the jurors with no food, water, heat or tobacco. When the jurors returned the same verdict two days later, the judge held them in contempt and ordered that each pay a fine. One refused to pay and another court – basing its decision on the belief that the jury ruled based on the *facts*, and not its interpretation (or nullification) of the law – held that a jury could not be punished simply because of the verdict it returned, assuming that the jury acted in good faith. Thus, the issue of whether a jury could find the law itself improper was studiously avoided.

As an aside, or perhaps not, William Penn later came to the United States and founded Pennsylvania, drafting a charter including liberties for a free and fair trial by jury and freedom of religion.

The story of John Peter Zenger is often cited as the earliest example of jury nullification in the United States. In 1735, he was the publisher of the *New York Weekly Journal*, which printed articles accusing New York's colonial governor of rigging elections, among other crimes. Zenger was taken into custody (he spent eight months in jail) and was charged with "seditious libel" – a crime. When the case finally went to trial, Zenger was acquitted – even though the act of printing the material was all that was necessary for the government to convict. You see, Zenger argued that he could not be found guilty because the statements he published were true. The jury agreed and, in effect, nullified the harsh law which would have found him guilty for printing what was, in fact, the truth.

There are those who argue that jury nullification is important – that in the nineteenth century it helped to bring an end to capital punishment for minor offenses; more recently, it helped to bring an end to prohibition, and the enforcement of unjust laws such as those that criminalized homosexual sex. The flipside – all white juries in the South who refused to convict those clearly guilty of beating black men and civil rights workers, as but one example.

Should a jury that has taken its oath to make "a true verdict" be permitted to ignore the law, if the law is producing what the jury believes to be an unjust result? Or must a jury decide based on the law before them and wait, perhaps even after the case is over, for the legislature to change the law?

THE STORY

Julian Heicklen, now 87 years old, may be jury nullification's most fervent advocate. And he has been arrested at least a dozen times, by his count, for his activities. A former chemistry professor at Penn State University and member of the Fully Informed Jury Association (FIJA) – his detractors might argue "nutty professor" – Heicklen would frequently stand outside courthouses handing out flyers which said, in effect, that jurors had the right to decide cases based, not on the law, but on what the jury believes the law should be.

Notably in 2010 –the most well-known of one of his many arrests – Heicklen stood outside the federal courthouse in the Southern District of New York, one of the busiest and highest-profile courts in America, with a sign that said, "Jury Info." He handed out brochures:

> The judge will instruct the jury that it must uphold the law as he gives it. He will be lying. The jury must judge the law as well as the facts.

Juries were instituted to protect citizens from the tyranny of the government. It is not the duty of the jury to uphold the law. It is the jury's duty to see that justice is done.

You may choose to vote to acquit, even when the evidence proves the defendant "did it," if your conscience so dictates.

Q: Once on a jury must I use the law as given by the judge, even if I think it's a bad law, or wrongly applied?

A: No. You are free to vote on the verdict according to your conscience.

So incensed was the government with Heicklen's activities, perhaps at the request of judges of the court, that it sent undercover FBI agents to pose as jurors and tape record what Heicklen told them as he handed out FIJA's "Primer for Prospective Jurors." The government concluded that Heicklen was distributing pamphlets and speaking to prospective jurors "urging jury nullification." He was indicted for the misdemeanor charge of "attempting to influence the actions or decisions of a juror of a United States Court" – jury tampering, in other words.

As one would guess, this is not the activity one thinks of when faced with jury tampering. A mafia boss paying jurors for a not guilty vote; or threatening the family of jurors for that same vote. That is the jury tampering the public and the courts see, when they see the crime at all.

What did Heicklen do? He stood outside a courthouse with a placard and some flyers. Was the government's decision to indict Heicklen a stretch, or overuse of the criminal process? Were Heicklen's actions protected by the First Amendment – freedom of speech? Heicklen thought so, and, representing himself, made a motion to dismiss the indictment.

From the government's point of view, one's free speech rights are tempered when they interfere with the judicial system. But Heicklen said he never interfered with the system, he merely made certain people knew their rights. Indeed, he never told a specific juror how to vote in any given matter. While he said, "vote your conscience," he never told a juror who had been selected for a marijuana case, "don't allow the government to get away with these arcane and oppressive drug laws."

The federal district court in Manhattan ultimately agreed with Heicklen. A person could only violate the statute when he knowingly attempted to influence a juror's decision in a specific case before the juror or in relation to a point in dispute between the parties in a case before that juror.

In Florida, however, Heicklen did not fare as well. During the same time period as in New York, Heicklen and another handed out FIJA pamphlets to prospective jurors on the courthouse grounds. Florida, however, had a specific administrative order governing conduct toward jurors, preventing the distribution of pamphlets like those Heicklen handed out. He was given copies of the order and asked to leave. He did not and was held in contempt. Heicklen appealed and the court concluded that, while the First Amendment applies to speech in public places, courthouse grounds are not "public." Thus, the State had a legitimate interest in controlling what was said or distributed on the steps of the courthouse and, in particular, making sure that all litigants had their day in court free from influences outside the courtroom.

DISCUSSION

We will never know how many instances of jury nullification actually occur in American courts. When a defendant is found not guilty, is it based on the facts or the way they were presented? Is it because witnesses were or were not believed to be truthful? Professor Heicklen is, thus, not the story about jury nullification – he is only the face of the story. Jurors don't require a Heicklen to explain what they are doing. Indeed, it may often happen that jurors who hold out for acquittal in the face of eleven votes to convict may simply tell their fellow jurors during deliberations that they don't believe a key prosecution witness. In fact, they may be voting to acquit – which will result in a hung jury (and, essentially, at least a temporary defeat for the prosecution) – simply because they "don't like" the crime being prosecuted.

But it can go much further. Hugo Black, a late Justice of the Supreme Court and a great believer in the jury system, used to tell this story.

Years ago, in the foot-hills of Alabama, a tenant-farmer was charged criminally with stealing a cow from his landlord, and was brought to trial. As was frequently the case in rural America, the jurors selected for the trial were acquainted with everyone, including the accused and his victim. Each juror knew that the landlord was a nasty bastard who tormented his neighbors, while frequently treating the town's orphans and widows with derision. By the same token, the tenant-farmer was the salt of the earth, beloved by everyone. But still, the evidence of his guilt was indisputable.

After the evidence was in and the jury retired to deliberate, it quickly returned to the courtroom to announce its verdict: "If the accused returns the cow, we find him not guilty." The judge was infuriated. His anger heightening, he commanded the jury to return to the jury room to deliberate – shrilly chastising them for their flagrantly "arrogant" and "illegal" verdict. Not a moment passed when they reappeared in the tensed courtroom to trumpet their new verdict: "We find the accused not guilty – *and he can keep the cow.*"

The American jury, Justice Black reminded his listeners, is effectively omnipotent in rendering an acquittal.

Now, the tenant-farmer story is lighthearted and possibly apocryphal. Few, today, however, would be particularly bothered by the "lawlessness" – if one can call it that – of the verdict reached by the jury in Justice Black's case: it talks about the theft of a cow, hardly the crime of the century, even though it is clearly not a victimless crime. But suppose a juror (or, for that matter, a jury), whether *counselled* by Professor Heicklen or even based on his own conscience chooses to ignore the judge's instructions in another type of case by voting to acquit because of a perceived need to "send a message" – e.g., to tell the police that certain conduct which occurred in the case was intolerable, even if the evidence of guilt was overwhelming.

Jurors bring, and should bring to the courtroom their own experiences – they have their own individualized thoughts about current events, war, community activities, societal norms and public opinion. And each juror is informed by what they have seen, read, and done.

So consider this speculation: an overwhelming majority of white America, who closely followed the case on television, believed that O.J. Simpson was actually guilty of the murders with which he was charged, while many black people in America (also avid viewers) perceived what occurred in a totally different way. Perhaps black people saw it that way because they were far more frequently the victim of police abuse in their communities. Put differently, they believed, while white Americans might generically not, that the police were simply capable of "playing with [blood] evidence" in a way designed to frame a defendant such as Simpson, even if they were framing him for something that he actually did. The Simpson jury, largely composed of minority members, might have been moved to acquit, not because O.J. was innocent, but because this was the time and place to "send a message" to the police, in a very loud and clear voice, that America, at least blacks in America, would no longer tolerate such police conduct.

To be sure, the Simpson jury might have fairly concluded that the blood evidence had been tampered with and that that evidence was critical to its verdict, or that prosecution witnesses, including one freely willing to use the "N" word, lied – jurors are perfectly entitled to make credibility judgments based on the experience that they bring to the table. But, suppose, a juror, jurors, or the jury actually concluded that the evidence was overwhelming against Simpson, but nonetheless decided, even without articulating it to anyone or among themselves, to acquit because they were so offended by the police conduct that the only way to deter it going forward was to acquit Simpson. Without question, that would be jury nullification of the most extreme or even worst sort – voting to acquit or actually acquitting notwithstanding the overwhelming evidence of guilt and the court's instructions where the crime is brutal murder.

Now, some (perhaps even Professor Heicklen) might argue that jury nullification is only a constitutional right on the part of jurors when the crime is victimless, and that is certainly not the case with murder. But does that mean a community so frequently abused by discriminatory law enforcement practices should not also have the right to send its message? Does the juror comply with his oath in nullifying when the crime is victimless, but not so when there is indeed a victim?

What of the converse – convicting the innocent? Suppose jurors feel that the *evidence* of guilt isn't sufficient, but the jurors heard testimony at the trial of other crimes committed by the defendant, even if the jury was told to consider that additional evidence only for limited purposes. And so, believing in a form of rough justice, they decide to convict (even without sufficient evidence), because in simple terms he's guilty of "something." Is that what Professor Heicklen and the FIJA bargain for when they support the rights of juries to nullify laws? After all, what's good for the goose should also be good for the gander, shouldn't it?

Now, no one truly argues that a jury should be able to "nullify" by voting to *convict* even if a conviction is not warranted by the evidence. Indeed, even those who support jury nullification as consistent with a juror's oath believe that conviction of a defendant who under the law should have been acquitted is intolerable. But countenancing a jury's ability to vote a case by deciding in a manner contrary to the weight of the evidence seems to enable a wholesale violation of the juror's oath, doesn't it?

Still, and although the oath a juror takes at the outset of a trial requires "a true verdict according to the evidence," serious scholars of the law and other commentators have opined, in no uncertain terms, that jury nullification is indeed a proper device to be employed by jurors in the appropriate case. FIJA has lobbied state legislators for statutes requiring courts to inform juries of the right to nullify. And the late Supreme Court Justice Antonin Scalia when asked at a Senate hearing about the role of juries in checking government power seemed open to the notion that jurors can "ignore the law" if the law "is producing a terrible result."

United States District Judge Jack B. Weinstein, the dean of the federal judiciary, while believing that jury nullification is rare and occurs only when there has been a breakdown in how justice is meted out in certain circumstances, has actually gone so far as to hail nullification as "one of the peaceful barricades of freedom." And indeed, even where courts have declined to instruct juries about the doctrine of jury nullification, they have acknowledged that "the pages of history shine on instances of the jury's exercise of its prerogative to disregard uncontradicted evidence and instructions of the judge." The Supreme Court, in fact, has recognized that judges have no recourse if juries acquit, even in the face of overwhelming evidence against the defendant. It has been said, however, that "a juror should not acquit unless he is firmly convinced that a gross injustice would be done by conviction . . . He must think that the actor was performing an act that was clearly justified or was exercising an undeniable moral right."

Northern jurors, in the distant past, courageously refused to convict "guilty" men who violated the fugitive slave laws. Yet, Southern jurors refused to convict those who murdered civil rights workers – a brand of jury nullification, to be sure. It is also, however, antithetical to the notion that jury nullification accomplishes a public good as a check on governmental power. Whether a law is good or bad, should be enforced or ignored is, let's face it, in the eye of a particular juror.

There is the deeply held American notion that juries perform an independent role in a system in which the people – not prosecutors, judges, or lawyers – have the last word. So, how, consistent with a juror's duty of honesty under his oath, may he occupy that independent role in having "the last word?" It presumably lies in his ability to address the concept of "reasonable doubt" when evaluating the evidence presented at trial. The way a court defines "reasonable doubt" may influence a jury seeking guidance on whether a case may be nullified. Courts have developed a series of definitions, all of which are guided in some degree by an effort to actually limit jury nullification.

One standard formulation includes the warning that a reasonable doubt "is not an excuse to avoid the performance of an unpleasant duty, nor the equivalent of sympathy, caprice, or 'whim'." Rather, reasonable doubt is often defined as "a doubt which would cause a reasonable person to hesitate to act in a matter of importance in his or her personal life."

As the definition of "reasonable doubt" is sharpened, however, the law contains traps which open doors to the possibility of nullification. For example, some courts choose to instruct juries that a reasonable doubt "is a doubt for which a juror can give a reason if he or she is called upon to do so in the jury room." Presumably, this instruction makes it more difficult for a would-be nullifying juror to hold out for acquittal on the basis of a doubt that is not based on a legal or evidentiary deficiency in the prosecution's case.

At bottom, we will never really know how many cases there are of jury nullification. Jurors may vote to acquit without stating their reasons and without pointing to the evidence or lack thereof. They are instructed that they "have no obligation to articulate the basis for their doubts" and there is considerable leeway for jurors to rest their decisions on collateral matters, such as those that lead jurors to nullify, irrespective of whether these matters supply a legal or evidence-based foundation to acquit.

This seems like so much gobbledygook. This formulation seemingly allows a juror to tell her fellow jurors that "I have a reasonable doubt" about the defendant's guilt and, as far as the law is concerned, she can basically elude the problem even if the basis for acquitting isn't truly "reasonable doubt," but rather an unwillingness to convict for a reason totally unrelated to guilt or innocence. It brings us ultimately to Aeschylus's aphorism that began this book – that the validity of an oath may depend more on the integrity of the oath-giver than the oath itself. The juror who seeks to nullify for reasons unrelated to the quantum and quality of the evidence presented at trial simply cannot be compelled to vote to convict and cannot be replaced as a juror for reflexively saying to her fellow jurors "I have a reasonable doubt."

Still, to the extent that the juror has available to him the escape hatch that allows him use of the phrase "reasonable doubt," it may very well be that, while jury nullification is typically discouraged by the courts, precisely how a juror chooses to comply with his oath and the duty that inheres in doing so may turn out to be a matter of conscience and nothing more (at least if the juror keeps his true motivation when he decides to himself).

Indeed, unlike many jurors who vote to acquit, claiming to their fellow jurors or, for that matter, to anyone, reasonable doubt, despite not having truly seen the evidence as inadequate, Professor Heicklen, to *his* credit, was willing to stand up for what he believed. He was willing to tell whoever would listen what was truly on his mind about the occasional shortcomings of the criminal justice system – even though his protest was limited to certain types of cases.

Judge Weinstein quotes favorably the view of one scholar, R. Kent Greenawalt, who essentially sees jury nullification as an "amelioration" of the criminal process – somewhat akin to pardon or amnesty by the executive, charge reduction by prosecutors, sentencing and directed verdicts by judges. Employing that view, do jurors violate their oaths when they use their votes to "make things right" anymore so than do judges who fiddle with their rulings to the same end? Professor Greenawalt says that "a jury's obligation to apply the law could be outweighed by its duty to do what is morally just in an individual case." A scholarly view, indeed. But if the professor's view is right – although many judges would disagree with it – how many jurors know about it? And shouldn't they? I believe we know what Professor Heicklen would say about that.

CHAPTER ELEVEN
THE SPOUSE

Roswell Gilbert

THE OATH

The wedding day. One of the best days of the couple's life. Friends, family. And the person each has chosen to spend the rest of their lives with. Maybe the couple wrote their own vows, but if not, they typically take an oath that goes something like this:

> I take [the other] to be my wedded husband/wife, to have and to hold, from this day forward, for better, for worse, for richer, for poorer, in sickness and in health, to love and to cherish, till death do us part.

These vows have been around for centuries and derive from the Sarum liturgical rites of medieval England. While such rites are long abandoned, the Anglican Church's *Book of Common Prayer*, published in 1549, was heavily influenced by the Sarum marriage vows, and this oath has remained largely unchanged. Not all religious ceremonies use just these words, yet the thoughts, with variations ("I vow to care for you as long as we both shall live"), have made their way into civil ceremonies. And, we must assume, even religions, and their members, which do not use these precise words, expect a married couple to comport with the general tenets of their religion which, in most cases, will mean being faithful to and honoring one's spouse.

"In sickness and in health." "Till death do us part." The words, the concepts, anticipate that the couple will be together forever; for the rest of their lives. Even if the life of one ends, by being together they will have fulfilled their vows, their oath to one another. But what of the oath when the life of one is cut short at the hand of the other? And does it make a difference if one took the life of the other because of debilitating illness – how does that comport with the promise to love in sickness and in health?

It's a more difficult question than one might think. Consider the story of Emily and Roswell Gilbert.

THE STORY

Roswell and Emily Gilbert were married for 51 years. Emily was suffering from Alzheimer's and osteoporosis, a degenerative bone disease. Her physician prescribed pain killers, but there is little doubt that she was in pain. She was confused. She told friends, "I am so sick. I want to die." But her prognosis was such that death was not imminent. She could live five, even 10 years. Neither illness brought her to death's doorstep.

By all accounts, Emily and Roswell were in love, even after 51 years. Toward their later years, she would walk the grounds of their Florida condominium community when he left their apartment to go to meetings, or to go to the pool. On March 4, 1985, they went to lunch, as they had done every day. Returning to their apartment, Roswell gave Emily her medicine and went to a meeting just downstairs. Emily left the apartment to look for him; she was confused. She found him at his meeting, where according to at least one account, she screamed,

"Please end my suffering. I want to die. Kill me." Roswell took her back to their apartment and helped her onto the sofa, where she begged, "Please, somebody help me."

Roswell knew she was in pain; he knew she was suffering. He also knew she would only get worse as the years wore on. All he could think was that he had to put her out of her misery. He did something many of us would find unthinkable – he went to the next room, took his gun from a drawer, and loaded a single bullet. He then returned to the living room and shot Emily, his beloved to whom he vowed to love in sickness and in health, in the head from behind so that, he later said, she would never see her death coming. As he held her hand after he shot her, he felt her pulse. Roswell then did something that may well have been his legal downfall – he went back to the other room, loaded another bullet into the gun and shot Emily a second time, making sure she was dead. Roswell did not run; he did not hide. He called the condominium's security guard and said, calmly, "I just killed my wife."

When asked, later, why he killed Emily in such a violent manner, Roswell said that he believed a gunshot was the most humane way for her to die – with a bullet, there is an instantaneous cessation of consciousness. With poison – even if Roswell knew where to get it or what dose to use – he might cause her to be sick, but not die. Roswell could not have sought advice about how to kill Emily from medical professionals. After all, they were obligated to treat, not end, suffering like Emily's. And putting her in a nursing home would have been the cruelest choice of all. They would have been separated and she would have been alone.

Roswell, critically, never spoke to Emily about killing her; he later testified that all he wanted to do was end her suffering, no matter the consequences. And that he did it for her.

Why do we know all this? Why do we know what was going through Roswell's mind as he decided to pull the trigger? Twice? Well, the consequences of his actions were great indeed. The State of Florida prosecuted Roswell Gilbert, then 75 years old, for the murder of his wife. And he was found guilty – euthanasia, "mercy killing," was simply not a defense. Emily was not on the threshold of death, which would have perhaps allowed her spouse to make a life-termination decision for her (although even if so, not one that permitted him to kill her with a gun). Simply, none of the legal exceptions – the defenses, if you will – applied to Roswell Gilbert.

More than that, the prosecutor – Kelly Hancock – argued to the jury that Roswell acted not to ease Emily's suffering, but rather his own. Hancock argued that Roswell acted out of selfishness, not love. The proof? That second bullet. And the jury – later interviewed – agreed. While the first bullet may have demonstrated that Roswell was overcome and distraught, the jury believed that the second bullet smacked of premeditated, indefensible murder.

So, at the age of 75, Roswell was sentenced to the minimum time allowed for murder under Florida's statutes – 25 years in prison. To remove his wife from her hell, he walked into his own. The Gilberts' only daughter broke down – she didn't want to see her father in jail, much less to see him die in jail. Yet, at the time, Roswell remained steadfast. After his conviction, he said: "I don't feel like I committed a crime at all. Justice is on my side, but the law is on somebody else's side." Years later he thought differently – he seemed to understand he should not have killed her.

After Roswell served five years, he was granted clemency and the governor commuted his sentence. Kelly Hancock, the prosecutor who convinced the jury to convict Roswell but who was then no longer with the prosecutor's office, petitioned on Roswell's behalf. Even though the system worked, Hancock felt Roswell had been punished enough: "His health is deteriorated, and I think his release puts to an end a very, very tragic case – a case that made us all more aware of the problems the sick and the elderly have." Simply, he did not believe the 25-year mandatory minimum was for situations such as this.

Roswell went on to live for another five years after his release and died at the home of his daughter.

DISCUSSION

Unlike other oaths, the marital vow – itself an oath – has no enforce-able efficacy. It is, rather, aspirational. Or maybe another expression of it is that the vow is intended to describe the spiritual essence of the relationship.

It is, for pragmatists, impossible to swear to love and cherish some-one *in futuro*, any more than it might be an oath to blindly and with-out question love and cherish God for the rest of one's life – ideal, but likely an impossible commitment. The dynamic of human interac-tion with one's spouse is far different than other legal relationships. Of course, going in, most couples plan to be together forever, but typically, especially for young couples, they don't even consider death or deadly illness when they begin their married lives together. They may think of ups and downs and even illness along the way, but not sickness that may cause them so much pain that they may want death to take them out of their misery. Nor sickness that may make them unable to watch their loved one suffer any longer.

When taking marital vows, most look at those vows as something other than formulaic expressions of devotion. By saying that they are with each other "for better or worse," a couple pledges a lasting com-mitment to one another. And, cynical as it might sound, while there might not be a better way to communicate the essence of that relation-ship, the vow is, in reality, only as good as the relationship continues to be. It may well be that a couple's decision to "renew" their vows may be seen as articulating that the feelings expressed long ago remain in effect despite the passage of time, and the realization by both that the

Sturm und Drang of life's journey among the waves has not diminished the commitment expressed by one another in times past.

And whether or not when they first married, Roswell Gilbert's vows contemplated an obligation to "stick with Emily" through thick and thin and throughout any sickness that might eventuate, a prosecutor could hardly seek to enforce that oath as an "obligation" as part of his prosecution of Roswell for Emily's murder. The mere fact that one violates the marital vow is certainly not, in and of itself, a criminal act. Yes, perhaps their daughter, their families or the community in which they lived might have found Roswell wanting if he violated his vow. What if he couldn't take it anymore and simply walked out on Emily as she remained in pain? Suing him for divorce (and their assets) would have been the available legal remedy for her. The ethical and legal obligations imposed, for example, on doctors, lawyers, or even journalists to comply with their oaths, simply don't apply to affairs of the heart – even when solemnly expressed and expressed in terms of a contract (of marriage).

Would we consider Roswell's actions the same way if Emily had announced, when she was fully competent (or *compos mentis*), to "shoot me when I can no longer be the person who I once was"? In that context, would Roswell have been acting on the vows they once took? Or would Emily have, in effect, "waived" the requirement that he adhere to those vows?

Yes, this was not a matter of a spouse pulling the plug. Euthanasia – and certainly death by gunshot – is against the law, and it wouldn't be any different if the "killer" was Dr. Jack Kevorkian (a messiah to some; the devil incarnate to others) or Roswell. Except that Roswell, of course, would be able to stand on more solid footing, inasmuch as he was, at least ostensibly, acting out of love – taking the bold action of killing Emily with the potential for prosecution.

But here's the curious thing. The prosecutor argued that significant proof of Roswell's criminal guilt lay in the fact that Roswell conceded that Emily never told him to kill her. Yes, of course, Roswell's defense, in the eyes of a jury, might have been more sympathetic if Emily had given an affidavit: "Please kill me and end my suffering." But maybe there's a different view. With his very freedom on the line, Roswell, who testified in his own defense, could easily have said "she begged me to shoot her." There would have been no countervailing witness to deny that, with Emily already in the grave.

It is interesting that in virtually every case involving a mercy killing by a spouse in the face of a painful disease, the surviving spouse states that the spouse specifically begged for death (the precise reason why the Gilberts were chosen for this discussion, rather than any other). Maybe, then, Roswell's refusal to perjure himself and put the onus on Emily's own stated desire to die was actually somehow proof of the integrity of his devotion in how he chose to comply with his marital vow.

If one looks at the likely spiritual nexus between Roswell and Emily at the outset of their relationship – that they would stick with each other for better or worse – perhaps for better or worse might mean doing the unthinkable, that is, pulling the trigger because he knew in his heart, as might no one else, what she would have wanted. And whether Emily uttered the words "shoot me," "kill me" or "put me out of my misery" immediately before the act in question, one might argue that he was truly with her "for better or worse" in a way he frankly knew would cause himself a hell on earth long after she was gone.

Did Roswell, indeed, actually fulfill his marital vow to Emily? We will never know.

AFTERTHOUGHT:

Putting aside the issue addressed above and lest it go unsaid, the nature of the marital relationship has evolved significantly in current times. The evolution is based in part upon the higher incidence of divorce, and that this likely goes into the thinking of couples considering marriage. But there are other considerations, for example, "open" and non-conventional marriages. For them, spouses may not see their counterparts as violating their oaths, as long as the offended spouse isn't embarrassed by the other's indiscretions.

Given these complicating factors and not intending to condone spousal oath violations, consider this scenario: a wife in an aging couple without children suffers from Alzheimer's disease. She barely recognizes her husband, and only occasionally. He takes care of her with every fiber of his being. But, still, he longs for companionship, physical and emotional, that she is incapable of. He seeks it out, or it just arrives at his doorstep. Does society, today, see him as violating his marital vows in the same way as in earlier times? And what does that say about the marital oath? Think about it.

EPILOGUE

To conclude, it is worth returning to the teaching of Aeschylus — that an oath is only as valuable, essentially binding, as he or she who takes it. In judging the worth of oaths, one wonders about the first oath in the Bible. The Bible and its teachings, of course, have had vast influence on the three great monotheistic religions and even most civil societies, which have adopted many of its regimens and protocols.

When the Patriarch Abraham was nearing death and wished to find a wife for his son Isaac in order to fulfill his legacy, he asked his loyal servant Eliezer (a Damascene) to travel to Canaan to find her, asking him to swear that he wouldn't choose from the daughters of the Canaanites. Eliezer placed his hand under Abraham's thigh, presumably as was the custom of the day, Abraham asking that Eliezer swear to *Abraham* concerning the matter. He did. In the oath, however, Abraham gave Eliezer an out, of sorts: "But if the woman will not follow you, you shall be absolved of this oath of mine." [Gen 24:5-9]. Eliezer abided by his oath and chose Rebecca (who was not a Canaanite) for Isaac.

But consider this: what if Eliezer was a lesser man, or a different kind of man? What if he was simply lazy? Or he wanted Isaac to marry his own niece, or the daughter of a friend – after all, Abraham was a wealthy man. So, theoretically, he could have never urgently searched for a "proper" wife for Isaac, and simply told Abraham, after a brief period of time, that no woman would follow him. Eliezer would be absolved of his oath to Abraham. In that case, what would have been the worth of Eliezer's oath?

In so many instances since the days of the Bible, people who have taken oaths have honored them precisely because they had *sworn to God*

– genuinely fearful that taking a false oath, and in the process invoking God's Name, violates the Third Commandment. Others, in civil society, have likewise genuinely feared the penalty of perjury, whether they placed their right hand on a bible and sworn or "affirmed" (as is more customary of oath takers today).

And so there stands Eliezer in his admirable uniqueness – whether one believes in God or not. He didn't swear to God – we actually aren't told by the Bible that he even believed in God – and he didn't swear to any regimen required by civil society. He simply swore to (or call it, promised) another man – in this case, his superior.

The oath, in Eliezer's case, as Aeschylus put it, was simply as noble as the man who took it.

ADDENDUM

Sources

THE CIA DIRECTOR AND WITNESS

Richard Helms, with William Hood, *A Look Over My Shoulder: A Life in the Central Intelligence Agency*, The Random House Publishing Group, 2003

Thomas Powers, "The Man Who Kept the Secrets: Richard Helms and the CIA," Alfred A. Knopf, Inc., 1979

Christopher Marquis, "Richard Helms, Ex-C.I.A. Chief, Dies at 89, *The New York Times*, October 24, 2002

Mark Lilla, Mark Moore, "The Two Oaths of Richard Helms," Harvard Kennedy School Case Program, January 1, 1983

THE LAWYER

North Carolina State Bar Grievance against Staples S. Hughes, February 6, 2007, File 07G0139

State of North Carolina v. Hunt, Petition for Writ of Certiorari, North Carolina Court of Appeals, From Cumberland County 85CRS16651-16654 (July 2007)

Debra Cassens Weiss, "PD Faces Ethics Complaint for Telling of Dead Client's Confession," *ABA Journal*, November 26, 2007

John Solomon, "Former N.C. Justice Takes Up Prisoner's Case," *The Washington Post*, November 28, 2007

Maurice Possley, "Inmate Freedom May Hinge on Secret Kept for 26 Years," *Chicagotribune.com*, January 19, 2008

Debra Cassens Weiss, "N.C. Drops Ethics Charges against PD Who Told of Dead Client's Confession," *ABA Journal*, February 5, 2008

"26-Year Secret Kept Innocent Man in Prison," *60 Minutes*, March 6, 2008

Adam Liptak, "When Law Prevents Righting a Wrong," *The New York Times*, May 4, 2008

Joel Cohen and Katherine A. Helm, "When a Lawyer Knows of Reasonably Certain Death," *law.com*, February 1, 2010

Spaulding v. Zimmerman, 263 Minn. 346 (Sup. Ct. Minn. 1962)

Swidler & Berlin v. U.S., 524 U.S. 399 (1998)

In re Miller, 584 S.E. 2d 772 (Sup. Ct. N.C. 2003)

Hunt v. Perry, 2016 WL 5416453 (E.D.N.C., Western Div. 2016)

THE MADE MAN

The Mob Museum, "Forty Years Ago, Jimmy 'The Weasel' Fratianno Turned On His Mob Family"

Michael J. Zuckerman, *Vengeance is Mine*, 1987

Peter Maas, *The Valachi Papers*, 1968

Ovid Demaris, *The Last Mafioso*, 1981

Joe Bruno, "Jimmy 'The Weasel' Fratianno," *Mob Rats*, 2014

Joseph Bonanno with Sergio Lalli, *A Man of Honor: The Autobiography of Joseph Bonanno*, 2013

THE CONSCIENTIOUS OBJECTOR

David Remnick, *King of the World: Muhammed Ali and the Rise of an American Hero*, 1998

Elijah Muhammed, *Message to the Blackman in America*, 1965

Nation of Islam, History

Clay v. United States, 403 U.S. 698 (1971)

THE PHYSICIAN

Edward Steers, Jr., *His Name is Still Mudd*, 1997

Douglas O. Linder, "The Lincoln Assassination Conspiracy," *The Great Courses, The Great Trials of World History and the Lessons They Teach Us*, 2007

Hippocratic Oath and *Hippocratic Oath, Modern Version*, History of Medicine Division of the National Library of Medicine

Maimonides Oath, Albert Einstein College of Medicine of Yeshiva University

THE PRESIDENT

Robert B. Stinnett, *Day of Deceit: The Truth About FDR and Pearl Harbor*, Touchstone, 2000

George Victor, *The Pearl Harbor Myth: Rethinking the Unthinkable*, Potomac Books, 2007

U.S. National Archives, "Pearl Harbor: Why Was the Attack a Surprise?" Presented by the Franklin D. Roosevelt Presidential Library and Museum

Report of the Joint Committee on the Investigation of the Pearl Harbor Attack,
    July 20, 1946

THE CITIZEN

Fred T. Korematsu Institute

Korematsu v. U.S., 323 U.S. 214 (1944)

Korematsu v. U.S., 584 F. Supp. 1406 (N.D. Cal. 1984)

Densho Encyclopedia

Charlie Savage, "Korematsu, Notorious Supreme Court Ruling on Japanese
    Internment, Is Finally Tossed Out," *The New York Times,* June 26, 2018

Trump v. Hawaii, 138 S. Ct. 2392 (2018)

THE CLERGY

Code of Canon Law §§ 983, 984

4 New Cath. Encycl., 133 (1967)

Morales v. Portuondo, 154 F. Supp. 2d 706 (S.D.N.Y. 2001)

Lightman v. Flaum, 97 N.Y. 2d 128 (2001)

People v. Phillips, (N.Y. Ct. of General Sessions 1813) reprinted 1 Western L. J.
    109 (1843) and 1 Cath. Law. 199 (1955)

THE JOURNALIST

O'Neill v. Oakgrove Construction, Inc., 71 N.Y.2d 521, 528 N.Y.S.2d 1 (1988)

N.Y. Civil Rights Law § 79-h

Branzburg v. Hayes, 408 U.S. 665 (1972)

Beach v. Shanley, 62 N.Y.2d 241 (1984)

Joseph C. Wilson 4th, "What I Didn't Find in Africa," *The New York Times*, July 6, 2003

Robert D. Novak, "Mission to Niger," *The Wall Street Journal*, July 14, 2003

Judith Miller, "My Four Hours Testifying in the Federal Grand Jury Room," *The New York Times*, October 16, 2005

cnn.com, "New York Times Reporter Jailed," October 28, 2005

Judge Reggie B. Walton, "United States v. I. Lewis 'Scooter' Libby," *Tough Cases*, New Press, 2018

Judith Miller, *The Story: A Reporter's Journey*, Simon & Schuster, 2015

Peter Berkowitz, "The False Evidence Against Scooter Libby,"*The Wall Street Journal*, April 6, 2015

Judith Miller, "AFTER THE WAR: UNCONVENTIONAL ARMS; A Chronicle of Confusion in the U.S. Hunt for Hussein's Chemical and Germ Weapons,"*The New York Times*, July 20, 2003

Nathan Siegel, "Our History of Media Protection,"*washingtonpost.com*, October 3, 2005

In re Grand Jury Subpoena, Judith Miller, 397 F. 3d 964 (D.C.C. 2005)

The New York Times Company v. Gonzalez, 459 F. 3d 160 (2d Cir. 2006)

THE JUROR

NYS Unified Court System Petit Juror's Handbook

Famous Trials by Professor Douglas O. Linder, at www.famous-trials.com

Joel Cohen, Katherine A. Helm, "The Illegality of Advocating for Jury Nullification," *law.com*, December 12, 2011

Paul Butler, "Jurors Need to Know That They Can Say No," *The New York Times*, December 20, 2011

Steven M. Witzel, "Jury Nullification In New York Cases," *New York Law Journal*, March 1, 2012

U.S. v. Thomas, 116 F 3d 606 (2d Cir. 1997)

James Joseph Duane, "Jury Nullification: The Top Secret Constitutional Right," 22:4 Litigation6-60 (1996)

Clay S. Conrad, "Jury Nullification: The Evolution of a Doctrine," Cato Institute, 2014

U.S. v. Heicklen, 858 F. Supp. 2d 256 (S.D.N.Y. 2012)

Bushel's Case, 124 E.R. 1006 (1670)

Schmidter v. Florida, Case No. 5D11-2588, 11-3036

Hon. Jack B. Weinstein, "Considering Jury 'Nullification': When May And Should A Jury Reject The Law To Do Justice," 30 Am. Crim. L. Rev. 239 (1993)

THE SPOUSE

R. Kent Greenawalt, "Conflicts of Law and Morality," 349-73 (1987)

UPI, *Chicago Tribune*, "Mercy Killing Trial To Hear Defense," May 9, 1985

William Plummer, "An Act of Love or Selfishness? the Friends of a Florida Wife Killer Depict Him as An Angel of Mercy,"*People*, May 27, 1985

Gilbert v. State, 487 So. 2d 1185 (1986)

Mercy or Murder? TV Movie, Release Date 1987

Brent Kallestad, AP, "Repentant Roswell Gilbert Freed for Wife's 'Mercy Killing'," August 2, 1990

Obituary, "Roswell Gilbert 85, Who Killed His Wife And Went To Prison," *The New York Times*, September 8, 1994

Scott Montgomery, Beth McLeod, "Shots in 1994 Fort Lauderdale Death Started Mercy Killing Crusade," *The Palm Beach Post*, September 9, 1994

www.ingramcontent.com/pod-product-compliance
Lightning Source LLC
Chambersburg PA
CBHW061326220326
41599CB00026B/5062